BACK IN THE SADDLE

BACK IN THE SADDLE
Your Complete Guide to Mature Biking

Olly Duke

Caring Books

© Olly Duke 2000

Published in 2000 by
Caring Books, PO Box 1565,
Glasgow G46 6SX
(Tel/Fax: 0141 571 0553)

Printed and bound in Great Britain
by Bell & Bain Ltd.

All rights reserved.

British Library in Cataloguing Publication Data.

Olly Duke asserts the moral right
to be identified as the author of this work.

This book is sold subject to the condition that it shall not,
by way of trade or otherwise, be lent, resold, hired out
or otherwise circulated without the publisher's prior consent
in any form of binding cover other than that in which
it is published and without a similar condition including this
condition being imposed on the subsequent purchaser.

ISBN 0-9523649-4-8

Book cover design by
Gourlay Graphics,
Suite 14 Dundas Business Centre
38 New City Road, Glasgow G4 9JT
(Tel: 0141 353 1211
Fax: 0141 353 0448)

Safety Notice

All the instructions and advice given in this book are based on reasonable research for accuracy. However, neither the publisher nor the author can control or be responsible for the way in which readers follow these instructions or advice. In particular (without limitations), neither the publisher nor the author can control or be responsible for the skill or otherwise of motor cycle riders, the condition and state of maintenance of their motorcycles and the condition of road surfaces.

Olly Duke

Olly is one of Britain's leading bike writers. Before going freelance in 1993, he was a features writer and road tester for Motor Cycle News. In addition to his weekly "Typical Biker" column in the Daily Telegraph's Saturday motoring section, he has contributed regular features to magazines, including Bike, RiDE, American Motorcycles, Auto Express, Top Gear, Motor Cycle News, Superbike, Performance Bikes, Maxim and other foreign bike magazines. Olly is also a talented cartoonist and his favourite biking character, Speedy Spike, appears frequently throughout this book.

He has ridden and road-tested a huge variety of racing bikes, including Carl Fogarty's championship-winning Ducati 916 and most current road bikes. He tutors at track days.

Olly was bitten by the biking bug when he was 14 - that's when he started riding mopeds - and since then has toured South Africa, Europe and much of the USA by bike. He lives in England with his partner and two young children. When he's not writing about bikes, touring, racing, or road-testing them, Olly can be found at weekends alongside his six-year-old son who now has a motorcycle of his own!

This book is dedicated to Joe Barr and my two little biking buddies, Jack and Ella. Also to Harry Heasman, who has to fight tooth and nail with his parents for the right to ride.

THANKS

To bespectacled Kieren Puffett for invaluable research, RiDE magazine for plentiful informative information, Dave Parkinson of Race Components for his technical expertise ("Hullo, Dave, it's me again...hello, are you there?") and the Daily Telegraph's Saturday motoring section for letting me adapt some of my Safer Riding column, used in chapters 11 and 12. Oh, and to my faithful and crazy hound Spike, who features so largely in the cartoons.

CONTENTS

Introduction:	Born-Again To Ride	1
Chapter 1:	Taking Your Test	5
Chapter 2:	Your Choice of Bike	12
Chapter 3:	Buying Your Bike	22
Chapter 4:	Dressing Up For Summer	30
Chapter 5:	Wrapping Up For Winter	40
Chapter 6:	The Law and Insurance	49
Chapter 7:	Where You Can Go	60
Chapter 8:	Touring The Great Unknown	69
Chapter 9:	Fast 'n' Furious: Track Days	80
Chapter 10:	Basic Maintenance	91
Chapter 11:	Basic Riding Techniques	102
Chapter 12:	Advanced Riding Techniques	118
Chapter 13:	Tuning Your Bike	137
Chapter 14:	Bits And Pieces: Accessories	146
Glossary		157
Further Reading		170
Index		171

Introduction

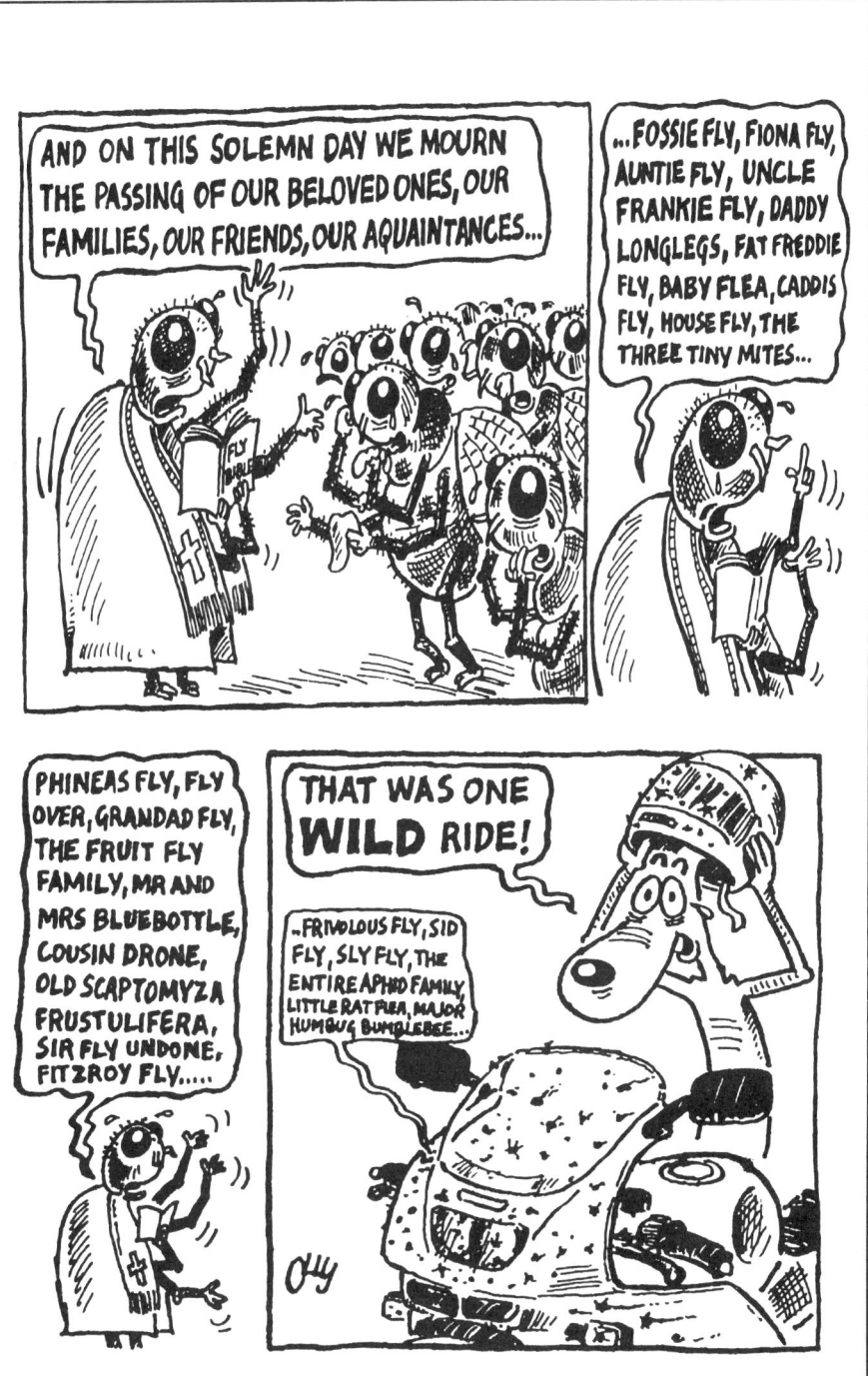

Introduction
Born-Again To Ride

"When I was sixteen I had a bike and I rode like crazy on it. Now I want to start biking again, but everything's changed. Bikes are so much bigger and faster. I don't know where to start, but I'm determined to get back in the saddle again."
David, 36 years.

The resurrection of the motorcycle in Britain over the past few years has been fuelled by people in their thirties and forties, who probably experienced the excitement of two wheels in their youth and want a taste of the good life once more.

An amazing 60 per cent of people, either returning to or getting involved in motorcycling for the first time, are over 30 years old, and well over 20 per cent of those are 40-plus. And it's not just men who are flocking to two wheels, it's women too. So when your mates chide you about trying to discover your lost youth, you now know you're not alone. Cynics might say this book is written by a sad old git, for other sad old gits. But the great thing is we know we're not sad old gits. We're the ones having the fun!

Back In The Saddle will tell you everything, from how to get a good deal when you're buying a bike to how to experience the thrill of the race track. We'll take you touring, advise you on how to grovel when you've been nicked for speeding, show you how to maintain your machine, and much more.

Bikes are thrilling. Bikes are freedom. Bikes are a way of life. In fact bikes are whatever you want them to be. They're emotive too. From the moment you shell out your hard-earned cash, your motorcycle is your pride and joy. That piece of machinery represents you. Whether you ride a rat bike, a race replica, a trailie or a cruiser, you're making a statement about yourself.

But the statement goes further. The gear you wear rubber-stamps the image, not just to other bikers, but to the rest of society as well. When you're kitted up and on the road, you're different. You're not like everyone else, encased in a tin box on wheels, dribbling along in a queue behind some slow-moving, godforsaken lorry.

Biking is not just a pose, it's also an art. It doesn't matter how well you think you can ride, you can always improve on your skills. And the better rider you are, the more pleasure you'll derive from motorcycling. Not only that, you'll be a safer road user too. Your life depends on it.

Why I Started Biking

I started riding because my parents, who lived in Switzerland, were stupid enough to give me a moped at the age of 14. For my folks, it was a way of getting me out of their hair; for me it was total freedom. I then rode a friend's ratty, oily BSA C15, complete with naff monkey bars and back-rest, and I was smitten. By the age of 16 the rot had set in and ever since then I've owned bikes.

I toured through Southern Africa, the States, and throughout Europe. At the age of 36 I decided I needed to race, so a friend and I bought a Norton Dominator combination, which we blew up in style at Donington Park (simply because we didn't know about gearing). I then progressed to solo racing and had eight crashes in my first year (simply because I thought that going fast meant cracking open the throttle at the earliest opportunity).

The ensuing years flew by, road testing and feature writing for various magazines, and now my six-year-old son has his first little off-road motorcycle. He's started taking his sister pillion, terrifies his mother and has inspired me to buy my first motocrosser, a Suzuki RM250, at the age of 47.

There's a big biking world out there and however old you are there's always more to explore. **Back in the Saddle** will help you get out and enjoy it!

Go On, Do It

Here are ten possible reasons why you haven't got back in the saddle:
1. You've lost your youthful sparkle
2. The cabbage patch at the bottom of your garden is your priority
3. You now weigh 16 stones
4. Fun? Oh yes, I remember...
5. You're stuck in a rut

6. That grey Mondeo is the car of your dreams
7. The double-glazing salesman did a great job...
8. And you also reckon you need a new fitted kitchen
9. You're worried what the neighbours will think
10. You're afraid the kids will laugh at you

......And here are ten reasons why you definitely should:
1. It's exhilarating
2. It's a challenge
3. You learn new skills
4. It's escapism
5. You meet new friends
6. Every journey is fun
7. It's a way of exploring the world
8. It makes you feel young
9. You're no longer stuck in traffic
10. It becomes a passion

Go on, do it! Get back in the saddle!

Chapter 1: Taking Your Test

1
Taking Your Test

"I'm completely confused about the licensing system for motorbikes. I've asked a few mates about how to go about taking a bike test and no-one seems to know the ins and outs. I've just picked up a leaflet explaining the situation and I'm still not sure what's the best thing to do."
Sandra, 36 years.

Even though you're a born-again biker, the chances are that you never bothered to take your test in your younger days. Now is the time to get your full licence. Passing your bike test may seem like a logistical nightmare at first. Gone are the days when you simply rode a leaky, underpowered four-stroke, a bored examiner asked a few questions about the Highway Code and then got you to ride round the block, after which you were probably qualified to ride whatever you wished.

Now you have to leap several hurdles to obtain the passport to full power: the Compulsory Basic Training (commonly referred to as the CBT and valid for three years), a Theoretical Test (a must if you don't have a full car licence, and valid for two years), and finally one of three Pursuit Tests. Fortunately, 70 per cent of riders pass their bike test first time, compared to 46 per cent of car drivers.

How Do I Start?

Hurdle 1: Provisional licence
All motorcyclists need a provisional motorcycle licence or a provisional motorcycle entitlement on their car licence. A full car licence carries an automatic provisional motorcycle entitlement; if you hold a provisional car licence you'll need to fill in form D1 (obtainable from a post office) to add the provisional motorcycle entitlement to your car licence. If you

do not pass the motorcycle tests within the two years, you lose your motorcycle entitlement for one year.

Hurdle 2: Compulsory Basic Training (CBT)
The CBT teaches you basic bike control and how not to get wiped out when you venture onto the road. The training generally only takes a day or two, on an off-road area such as a car park or school playground, and is followed by a test. Bikes are usually provided by the training school, and are 125cc, 12bhp machines. The pass rate is around 95 per cent, depending on the training school. Once you have your CBT Certificate (Certificate DL196), you're allowed to get your hands on a wheezy, 14.6bhp 125cc with L-plates. You're not allowed to carry a pillion or ride on motorways. The CBT certificate is valid for three years, during which time you must take and pass the Theory and Pursuit Tests if you want to progress to the bike of your dreams.

Hurdle 3: Theory Test
There's no need to take this if you hold a full car or moped licence. You will be asked 35 multiple-choice questions in 40 minutes to assess your knowledge of the Highway Code and driving-related matters, and you must answer at least 28 questions correctly. The pass rate is 90 per cent, but watch out for the trick question. The exam is held at one of 140 test centres and you can sit it on weekdays, evenings and Saturdays. You must pass the Theory Test before applying for your Pursuit Test.

Watch out for the trick question...

Hurdle 4: Pursuit Test
This is similar to the car test, except that the examiner will follow you either in a car or on a bike, relaying instructions via a two-way intercom. You'll be assessed on your safety around town and on your bike control. You'll also have to answer a question on how a pillion affects the balance of a bike and you must demonstrate your ability to manoeuvre a bike while walking alongside it. There are now three types of licence you can qualify for, determined by your age and which type of bike you take the Pursuit Test on. Read on...

Which Motorcycle Licence?

Full Licence: The Direct Access route gives you carte blanche to ride any capacity, any power machine. It's by far the most popular test route, but you must be over 21 and take your Pursuit test on a bike of 47bhp or more.

A Licence: This qualifies you to ride bikes of up to 33bhp, with a power-to-weight ratio of not more than 0.16kW/kg (that's technical jargon for 'pretty damned slow'). After two years you automatically graduate to a full-power licence, and if you're under 21 this is your favoured option. You take this Pursuit test on a 125cc, 14.6bhp machine.

A1 Licence: Follow this route and you'll be stuck on 125cc machines that pump out a measly 14.6bhp. Here, your Pursuit test is taken on a 75 to 120cc bike that cannot exceed 62mph. Avoid this route at all costs.

Now For Some Training...

Even if you're cock-sure you don't need training because you think you remember it all from your younger biking days, the fact is you do. You must leap those hurdles in the way the examiner expects, so your first job is to find a training school. There are two nationwide organisations, the CSM (a professional business that runs seven days a week) and the BMF (run by the riders' rights organisation, which uses unpaid volunteers). There are also local training schools that can be found in the Yellow Pages, while most bike dealers have details of the nearest training schools. Failing that, you can contact the Driving Standards Authority (0115 901 2595) for information. When selecting a training school, ask yourself the following questions:

How do I know the training school is any good?
1. Ask for their pass rate on the CBT and Pursuit Test. The CBT pass rate should be around 95 per cent and the Pursuit Test pass rate should be about 70 per cent.
2. At least one instructor at the school should hold a C-licence, which looks like a yellow credit card and is given after the instructor has passed a course run by the DSA. The other instructors should have been trained by the C-licence holder.
3. Go along and watch. See how the students get on and talk to them about the tuition. Good feedback bodes well.
4. Ask what facilities the organisation offers. For example, the CSM will hire out clothing, helmet and bike, the BMF hires out bikes, while others will hire out a bike and provide the clothing free.

What training is on offer?
Everyone needs to be trained for the CBT, but beyond that there are various options:
Intensive Course: If you're desperate to sling your leg over a full-power machine, this is a quick, one-hit choice. It consists of courses lasting up to six days, with the test booked for the end of the training. How much, or how little experience you have will determine the length of the course you need. The instructor/pupil ratio should be no more than 1:5 and you can expect to pay around £400 for a six-day course, which includes the CBT, bike hire and tuition.
Residential Course: This is an intensive course, but you stay at the training school. Some schools offer after-hours thrills such as karting, but you're more likely to stay in a caravan than a five-star hotel.
Weekly Course: The advantage of this route is that it's less intensive than the other two, as you learn week by week. It's crucial not to let lessons slip, as you can quickly go off the boil and forget what you've been taught. You apply for the Pursuit Test as and when you're ready.

What else can training schools provide?
Clothing: Most training schools provide the basic essentials for riding a bike, including helmet, gloves and waterproofs. If you've already got the biking bug, it's worth kitting yourself out properly with your own helmet, boots, gloves, and leather jacket and jeans. You can buy additional gear as you progress and find out what you need.
Bikes: Most learners take the Direct Access route, so there's little point

in buying a 125 just to learn on. Training schools normally loan a small-capacity machine for the CBT and then a machine suitable for the Direct Access Pursuit test (one more powerful than 47bhp). Most schools loan these out on an hourly basis, but first make sure you are insured to ride them.

<u>Extras</u>: Some of the bigger training schools can provide rolling roads and smaller automatic bikes for nervous riders.

A Brief Recap....

Bear in mind the following facts when you are about to decide on training and the test itself:

- If you hold a full car licence you can ride a moped on the road (after completing the CBT) without L-plates.
- If you pass your test on an automatic bike, then you can only ride automatic bikes (in other words scooters).
- Your full car licence acts as a provisional motorcycle licence. If you have a provisional car licence, you need to obtain form D1 from the post office (which you send to the DVLA) for the motorcycle entitlement to be added.
- The next step is to find a qualified training organisation by looking in the Yellow Pages, asking at your local bike dealers, or contacting the Driving Standards Agency.
- You'll know if the trainer is qualified because at least one instructor should hold a C-licence, while the other trainers should have been trained by a C-licence holder in the same organisation.

- You can do the CBT and Theory Test in any order, but you need to pass the Theory Test before applying for the Pursuit Test.
- The Pursuit Test is broken into three categories: the Direct Access route to a full licence, the A-licence route that entitles you to ride any 33bhp bike, and the A1 licence route that permits you to ride 125cc machines with a power output of no more than 14.6bhp.
- If you choose the Direct Access route, you can ride 47bhp-plus bikes on the road with L-plates, but you must be accompanied by a C-licence holding instructor.
- The best way to get into biking is to pass the CBT on a training centre's 125, take the Theory Test, have an intensive three-day (or longer) course on a 47bhp-plus bike, and finally take your Pursuit Test. It's the expensive option, but it's worth it.

And Finally...

If you've just passed your test, or are returning to biking after a number of years, seriously consider taking an advanced riding course. Your driving licence provides you with only the most basic skills. You'll still need to know how to corner properly, how to overtake, how to look out for dangerous situations in town, and a host of other survival techniques.

What's more, the greater your skills, the more you'll enjoy your riding. You'll be smoother, faster and far more controlled. You won't find yourself in heart-stopping situations and, if you do, you'll know how to get out of them.

By taking advanced lessons, your instructor will stamp out bad habits before they develop, you'll learn in weeks what might otherwise take years, and you'll have the chance to discuss ideas. Most of the motorcycle magazines carry adverts for advanced tuition. You ideally want to learn from a RoSPA instructor, as they are the most highly qualified.

You should also read avidly. Chapters 11 and 12 of this book give some tips on how to improve your riding, although they are by no means comprehensive. *Motorcycle Roadcraft, the Police Rider's Handbook* (an HMSO publication) may be predictably dull, but it contains essential information and is available from main bookshops. American race instructor Keith Code's *Twist of the Wrist* (Vols I and II) is for the more cerebral, advanced rider, but is superb nevertheless.

Chapter 2: Your Choice Of Bike

2
Your Choice Of Bike

"I found it a complete nightmare trying to choose the right bike for me. There are so many styles, so many engine sizes, it's hard to know where to begin. I felt that the salesman was trying to push me into buying something I didn't particularly want."
Mike, 34 years.

Just look in the classified ads and you'll see loads of virtually brand-new, low-mileage bikes for sale. One reason for this is that people buy the wrong machine. They find that their motorcycle is too fast, or too slow, or plain uncomfortable. This costs money – they lose out on the miles they've clocked up, on depreciation, and have the hassle of selling it. They then have two choices: drop out of motorcycling altogether, or hunt around for something else.

Making a decision

Deciding which bike to buy can be a nightmare. There are so many makes and types, so many images. You want to be a World Superbike champion? Buy a Ducati 916. You want to be an urban cowboy? Then go the whole hog, splash out on a Harley-Davidson. You want to be a sand-busting, Paris-Dakar hero? Think about a big trailie.

Before you walk into the showroom, decide what type of bike is right for you. Think seriously about your biking experience, what you intend doing with your machine and how you want the world to see you. Don't just buy the latest all-singing, all-dancing crotch rocket because your mate has one – that could be a painful mistake.

Ask yourself a few questions. For instance, do you want to go touring? Or do you fancy sports riding? Or do you need a machine for commuting as well as for pleasure? Or would you rather indulge in some gentle cruising? Talk to other people who own bikes to find out what they get out of them, and read the test reports in the magazines. By the time you walk into the showroom, you should have a pretty good idea of what you want from motorcycling.

Here's a brief summary of the main categories of machines on offer. There are hundreds more bikes available, but this should point you in the right direction:

1. "Big Boys' Toys" – Large-Capacity Sportsters

These are the bikes with the speed, power, handling and glamour that have led the recent boom in the bike market. They're the ones that give that massive adrenaline rush every time you twist the throttle, and they come with all the cutting-edge technology money can buy. Most people returning to two wheels go for them.

More Honda FireBlades have been sold since the bike hit the showrooms in 1992 than anything else and they are incredibly fast. Big-bore sportsters have blistering acceleration. There isn't a car on the road that can stay with them. If you haven't the experience to handle 150bhp, sharp brakes and cornering ability that at first appears limitless, think seriously before you shell out that money. Many people buy these bikes, find them absolutely terrifying – and then sell them on. Machines such as Yamaha's R1 and Kawasaki's ZX-9R, which compete with the FireBlade, are in a league of their own. But all this sportiness entails compromises, like their riding position, poor luggage-carrying capacity and limited weather protection. Typcially, they're not easy to ride in town and they only come into their own at high speed, so watch out for your licence.

But if you're confident you can handle the performance, there's nothing to beat them. The sheer thrill of opening up a ZX-9R, or swooping through a bend on the nimble R1, is something to behold. If you are reasonably fit (and don't have a bulging beer gut) you'll soon adapt to the lean-forward riding position too. They're a hoot on track days and, if you're in the right frame of mind, they also make excellent tourers. Sod the luggage – just head for those Alpine passes!

2. "Fast 'n' Furious" – 600 Supersports

Six hundred cubic centimetres of motor and 100bhp may not sound much, but this class is one of the most fiercely-contested, both on the race track and in the showrooms. Honda, Kawasaki, Yamaha, Suzuki and now Triumph all produce rip-snorting 600s that are capable of lapping race circuits faster than their 1000cc peers. The reason is simple: their power is easier to control and they are more nimble.

In reality they're just as quick on the road too, but without all that daunting performance. They have good suspension and brakes, and corner with gusto, but lack the aura of their big brothers. However, as a first buy for the born-again biker, they can make more sense. Honda's CBR600, Triumph's TT600 and Kawasaki's ZX-6R are extremely comfortable, while Yamaha's R6 and Suzuki GSX-R600 have more radical riding positions. The main drawback of 600s is that they don't have the wonderful mid-range power of the 1000cc pack. Ducati's 748 V-twin, which competes alongside the Japanese 600-fours in the Supersport race series, is the classy option, but its single-minded, race-honed attitude means it's not an everyday machine.

3. "Budget Biking" – Economy 600s

If you want decent handling, a good turn of speed and a bike for everyday use – all at a knockdown price – then this is the right class for you. The economy 600s don't have the glamour of their peers, but they are practical and pretty quick on the road. Suzuki kicked off the idea of the budget 600 when it produced the Bandit. It was the soft option to the Supersports class, with a less powerful engine, less aggressive brakes, lower-quality suspension and no full fairing. But it was a huge success, because it provided big laughs for little money. Honda and Yamaha have since jumped on the bandwagon with the Hornet and Fazer, and Suzuki now has the V-twin SV650.

If you're new to biking, these machines are well worth considering. Just a little over £4000 buys you heaps of fun and sensible biking, and the ability to tour, commute, scratch and carry pillions in comfort. Budget 600s are easy to ride too, with a potential cruising speed of over 100mph and acceleration that won't scare the pants off you.

4. "Dedicated Race Replicas" – 750s

The 750s were, until recently, the premier sports bikes. The World Superbike grids are full of these single-minded, head-down machines. Then along came the FireBlade, R1 and ZX-9, which sold for much the same money, were lighter and of course far more powerful. Now even 600 Supersports rival 750s in terms of performance, so they've been relegated to also-rans, with the exception of Suzuki's fabulous GSX-R750.

But 750s still have a faithful following. The Kawasaki ZX-7R, although a bit long in the tooth, is widely regarded as one of the best-looking sports bikes, while Suzuki's GSX-R750 is a complete headbanger.

5. "Alternative Sportsters" – V-Twins

The V-twin has been around for years, but it's thanks to Ducati that the big-capacity, twin-cylinder engine is now so highly regarded. V-twins deliver bundles of mid-range power, don't need revving hard to make them perform, and sound and feel unique. Ducati's success with its 916 was too much for the Japanese factories to bear. Here was a bike that looked sensational, won World Superbike championships and managed to combine the feel of a traditional bike with up-to-date technology. Although Honda and Suzuki have been reasonably successful with the VTR1000 and TL1000, nothing can match the might or styling of the Italian marque. However, the Japanese machines score with ease of use and reliability.

Big-capacity V-twins are the sensible alternative to multi-cylinder sports bikes. They get you out of the rat-race, they don't tempt you to do silly speeds, yet they're still great fun to ride. While the 916 and SP-1 are the nearest things you can buy to a racer on the road, the VTR1000 and TL1000S are sensible road bikes while the racy TL1000R makes a compromise between the two. Aprilia's stylish RSV Mille is softer than the Ducati and makes a more comfortable everyday machine, while you might consider Moto Guzzi's 1100 Sport Injection for something completely different.

6. "Go-Faster Mile-Munchers" – Sports-Tourers

As their generic name suggests, these large machines combine an element of sportiness with real comfort and the ability to tour effortlessly. And although they are powerful, they are extremely easy to ride. They excel at scything across the Continent, and leaving you feeling great at the end of a day in the saddle.

When Kawasaki brought out the ZZ-R1100 in 1990, it spawned this new class of bike. Since then Honda launched the CBR1100XX Blackbird, while Suzuki brought us its 195mph Hayabusa and Hawasaki its ZX-12. The ZZ-R and Blackbird, both capable of clocking around 185mph, are streamlined, wonderfully comfortable and make excellent trans-Continental mile-munchers. And although they don't provide race track-style handling, they can still bring a grin to your face.

The Suzuki GSX1300R Hayabusa is somewhat different. Its sporty riding position and lack of wind protection while sitting upright make it good for one thing...going at 200mph, a speed that is breathtaking. Kawasaki's ZX-12 is equally fast, but it has a more protective fairing and is much more comfortable.

7. "Muscle Bikes" – Big Retros

These are 'real' bikes, ridden by 'real' men – or that's what they're cracked up to be. Their meaty engines, stripped-to-the-skin styling and rip-snorting appearance are a little deceptive, because you don't need bulging biceps to ride one, and they actually make useful everyday machines. And as they are generally unfaired, a tolerable cruising speed is about 80mph.

If you are not fussed about weather protection, last-gasp braking or knee-down antics, big retros are excellent bikes. They are extremely comfortable, so long-distance touring on them is a pleasure, and they make good commuters. Suzuki's GSF1200 Bandit is superb value-for-money, Yamaha's XJR1300 is about as butch as you can get and Kawasaki's ZRX1100 is a traditionalist's dream.

MUSCLEBIKES...FOR REAL MEN...

8. "Dirt-Busters" – Big Trailies

Although trail bikes are popular on the Continent, they've never caught on in Britain. Big trailies tend to be tall and narrow, with wide handlebars and high seats, giving you an excellent view of the road ahead. Their heritage is rooted in Paris-Dakar type races, which run over Tarmac, rough roads and sandy deserts.

But despite their lineage, they make very good all-rounders, although short people might find their weight and height daunting. Honda's Varadero, Triumph's Tiger, and Cagiva's Elefant 900 and Gran Canyon 900 make superb tourers with some dirt road potential – but they're too cumbersome to tackle serious off-road challenges.

9. "Armchair Mile-Munchers" – Tourers

If your idea of fun is cruising the Continent in style, with unequalled luggage-carrying capacity and in superlative comfort, you should consider a big tourer. These weighty machines are deceptively quick and handle better than they should. They have enormous fairings, sculpted saddles, integrated luggage systems and often come with pillion backrests, sophisticated sound systems and air cooling vents!

BMW has cornered the market with its superb R1100RT and humungous K1200LT, but Honda's sporty ST1100 Pan European is easily an equal and Triumph's Trophy 1200 is not far behind. The ultimate armchair tourer is Honda's mighty GoldWing, which has become something of a cult machine.

10. "Bandannas 'n' Shades" – Custom Bikes

So you've seen the film Easy Rider and you know what custom bikes are about. All right, so Peter Fonda's was really a home-brew chopper with a Triumph engine, but he set the scene. Customs and cruisers are laid-back, feet-forward machines with wide bars, acres of chrome, throbby engines and more pose than you can shake a stick at. Harley-Davidson has stolen the limelight with its traditionally-designed, V-twin machines, but the Japanese are desperate for some of the action.

The painful truth is that anyone who buys a Japanese custom secretly wants to ride a Harley-Davidson. Harley technology may be rooted in the distant past, but that's its special appeal, and something the Japanese have been unable to mimic. The unique feel of a throbby Harley engine and the subtle, very traditional styling of its bikes, makes for an exceptional riding experience. While you know the Oriental customs will start every time at the push of the button, they are too refined and usually too gaudy to cut the mustard.

11. "British Beef" – Triumphs

Triumph deserves a separate mention, not because of any patriotic drum-banging, but because its bikes are subtly different from the run-of-the-mill stuff. The marque lives both on its heritage and its ability to survive while not competing head-on with the Big Four manufacturers. And when you buy into Triumph, which doesn't relentlessly update its bikes year-on-year, you drop out of the rat race.

Triumphs are not at the cutting edge of technology. Even though the firm's premier sportster, the three-cylinder 955i Daytona, can't compete with its Japanese counterparts, it still offers good performance, plus heaps more character. Triumph also produces tourers, sports-tourers and a trailie, but its staple diet is classic-looking machines like the Thunderbird. Its TT600 is Triumph's first attempt at muscling into direct competition with the Japanese.

12. "Plain Janes" – Middleweight Commuters

If many people are honest with themselves, a 500cc commuter is all they'll ever need. They can cruise happily at 90mph, they have a reasonable turn of speed and they're acceptably comfortable. Unfortunately these little twins have all the glamour of a train spotter in a crumpled anorak. Honda attempted to raise the profile with its CB500 race series, but still nobody (except train spotters) wants them.

The CB500, Suzuki GS500 and Kawasaki ER-5 produce a little over 50bhp, are softly-suspended and have average brakes, but they do make competent, everyday road bikes. They are light and easy to ride and, if you're new to motorcycling, are definitely sensible, entry-level machines. They're very easy to control, yet are just fast enough to bring a smile to your face. And if you've ever seen a well-ridden CB500 racer (no engine tuning or suspension mods allowed) you'll be amazed at what some people can do with them.

13. "Twist 'n' Go" – Scooters

Liam Gallagher rides one, Chris Evans commutes on one and a host of other stars and wannabes use them for posing on. While sports bikes are all the rage, there's been another, quiet, two-wheeled revolution taking place. Scooters have become big news again. Once the preserve of Mods in parkas, scooters are now aimed at everyone from stars to the starry-eyed. Their designer bodywork, ease of use and traffic-busting potential means they're a must for urban dwellers.

This new generation of scooters makes life easy. The machines have no gears, just a twist-and-go throttle with an automatic clutch and a variable pulley arrangement, plentiful storage space under the seat (enough for some shopping or a full-face helmet) and lockable compartments for sun glasses, gloves and the like. The 50cc scooters are capable of 30mph and can be ridden on a car licence, while a 100cc scoot will do 60mph and the 400cc scooters are genuinely capable of 80mph and comfy Continental cruising. The biggest-seller in Britain is Peugeot's sleek Speedfight 100, which costs just over £2000.

Helping You Decide

The choice is yours, but try our guide below to help you in your quest for the machine that's right for you. If you want:

- mind-boggling power, great handling...consider a big-bore sportster.
- razor-sharp handling, useful power...consider a Supersport 600.
- cheap, easy to use, and decent performance...consider a budget 600.
- fine handling, exciting engine, and race-replica looks...consider a 750.
- a bit of character, a broad spread of power... consider a V-twin.
- to tour (fast), comfort, sporty handling... consider a sports-tourer.
- something muscular, no frills, and lively... consider a big retro.
- to stand out from the crowd, tour, commute... consider a big trailie.
- to tour in luxury, listen to music, eat miles... consider a big tourer.
- to feel cool, do some cruising, turn heads... consider a custom bike.
- to commute, have fun, be economical... consider a 500cc commuter.

Chapter 3: Buying Your Bike

3
Buying Your Bike

"I know what sort of bike I want, but I don't know where to begin. A new, official import seems the sensible option, but a friend got a really good deal with his parallel import. There are also loads of ads for nearly-new machines too, which would be a big saving. Grey imports seem like too much of a grey area."
Richard, 48 years.

Making up your mind about which bike to buy is hard enough. And once you've poured through the road tests and plumped on Mr Right, you then have a bewildering choice of alternatives. Do you go for a new machine, or a parallel, or a grey import, or something second-hand? There are pros and cons to each, so have a good think before you part with your cash.

Official Imports

There's never been a better time to buy a new bike. The sales war between the parallel and official importers over the past few years has forced down the price of official imports, while the Big Four (Honda, Kawasaki, Suzuki and Yamaha) have also introduced numerous buying incentives. There was a stage when a new parallel could be up to £2000 cheaper than  an official import, but those massive differentials have largely disappeared and the market has stabilised. The differential between the two can now be as little as £500, so the price is only part of the equation.

For most people an official import offers peace of mind. The bike will come with a manufacturer's warranty, there are no questions hanging over its authenticity or roadworthiness, and the main manufacturers offer all sorts of after-sales benefits, such as automatic club membership, free rider training, discounted track days and preferential loan rates. It's certainly worth finding out what's available, because the after-sales benefits of buying an official import can far outweigh the saving you may make by buying parallel.

Dealers will also discount, so if you're after a Honda, for example, ring round your nearest Honda dealers to find out which one will give you the best price. But again, money is not the only criterion. While one dealer may be willing to discount the bike you're after, another may be willing to do a deal on clothing, after-sales servicing, or offer a free loan bike while yours is being serviced. Alternatively, you may feel that even though your local dealer doesn't come up with the best overall offer, it's worth buying from him simply because he's nearby. Finally, make sure you're quoted the on-the-road price, as the pre-delivery inspection (PDI) alone can cost over £200.

Parallel Imports

Parallels have made a huge impact on the bike scene, accounting for up to 20 per cent of total new sales. During the mid-1990s, official imports were selling at premium prices and demand for them far outstripped the supply. The parallel importers stepped in, offering identical machines to the ones sold by the official importers, but at hugely discounted prices.

This drove down the prices not just of official bikes, but of second-hand machines as well. The truth was exposed: we Brits had been paying well over the odds for the pleasure of two wheels.

The fly in the parallel ointment was the emergence of the cowboy dealer. Suddenly every man and his flea-bitten dog saw a quick buck in importing a few bikes.

They were flogging them off from the back of their garages, and the industry appeared to be spiralling out of control. To ensure their credibility, the main parallel importers set up the Association of Parallel Importers (API), whose members abided by a code of conduct. The API made sure its members' bikes conformed to European legislation, that warranties were made available and that a standard of after-sales service was established.

The most common parallels were (and still are) Hondas, largely because of the surplus of stock in Europe, the shortage of supply in Britain and the marque's popularity. Ducatis were also successfully parallel-imported, selling for up to £2000 less than their official counterparts, while other makes were also brought in, but in far fewer numbers. Naturally the majority of parallels were from Europe, although some were brought in from other countries like the United States.

Parallels are commonly imported with kilometer-per-hour speedometers and headlamp lenses designed for riding on the right-hand-side of the road. Normally the dealer will add mph stickers to the speedo and change the headlamp lens to make the bike road-legal for Britain. There are companies that will recalibrate both conventional and digital speedos for as little as £30, while some dealers will do the job free when asked. Despite the howls of protest from the official importers about the standard of PDI checks made by parallel importers, you can safely assume that a dealer belonging to the API will know how to put a bike on the road without endangering your life.

There's also been a huge fuss about the legality of parallel imports, which is little more than a smokescreen. Components such as indicators and silencers may not be technically legal (because they will not be EU certified if the bike comes from outside Europe), but neither is the law going to come down on you like a ton of bricks. What you must look out for, however, is whether the engine has been restricted. Some European countries and states in America impose a 100bhp limit – and the last thing you want is a gutless FireBlade!

If you do decide to buy parallel – and there are still some great bargains to be had – buy from an API-approved dealer. The dealer will be able to offer a warranty (all European bikes are theoretically covered by the manufacturer's warranty anyway) and the service back-up you'd expect from an official dealer. Just don't expect your local official dealer to jump at the chance of servicing your machine, however.

Grey Imports

If you want something different, like a screaming 400cc crotch rocket, you should think about a grey import. These are second-hand Japanese bikes that have been imported to Britain. Because of the licence and insurance regulations, 400cc bikes are plentiful in Japan, and you can find everything from a Kawasaki ZZ-R250 to Honda's mini-RC30, the gorgeous NC30. The more glamorous 400s (like the NC30, Kawasaki's ZXR400 and Yamaha's FZR400) have been officially imported to Britain, but they were very expensive and the class never took off. However, grey importers found a tidy niche in the market for low-mileage, good-condition and well-priced 400s. For example, a little over £3000 will buy you a mint NC30, a stunning little performer.

Buying a grey import doesn't come completely hassle-free, so check the following:
- The 400s are speed-restricted to 112mph in Japan, so if you want a full-power machine you'll have to ask the importer to derestrict your bike. If you decide to derestrict your machine after you've bought it, the job can cost up to £80.
- All bikes will have kph speedos, with mph stickers added by the importer. This is perfectly legal, but there are firms that will alter them to mph.

- Many greys arrive in Britain with noisy, aftermarket silencers, which will not pass an MoT. You're best off buying a bike with a standard exhaust system.
- While grey importers keep a good stock of the more common parts, you may have to wait for a few weeks for parts specially ordered for you from Japan, unless you pay to have them flown to Britain. The best greys to buy are the ones that have been officially imported to Britain, as parts are more readily available.

Getting It Right

Here is my 10-Step Guide To Buying Your New Bike:
1. Be certain which bike you want. Read the road tests in the motorcycle mags and try out a dealer's demo.
2. Find out what packages the different importers have on offer. This may influence which model you choose.
3. Many dealers will discount, so take advantage. Phone different dealers to find out which one gives the best deal.
4. Discounting the price of the bike is only part of the equation. If a dealer won't discount, he may do a deal on accessories or servicing.
5. If you are taking out a loan, shop around.
6. You may live some distance from the dealer you're buying from, and you may need a loan bike while yours is being serviced. Find out if one's available.
7. Run the bike in as recommended by the manufacturer. Thrashing a new machine can be detrimental in the long term.
8. Have the bike serviced as recommended, otherwise it will affect the warranty.
9. If you intend tuning your bike, find out how this affects the warranty.
10. Shop around for the best insurance deal. You'll be amazed at the varying quotes you're given.

Second-Hand

There's a very strong argument never to buy new. It's simple – and a glance at the classifieds will confirm it. Why pay the full price when there are thousands of immaculate, low-mileage bikes for sale (still covered by warranty) that are over a grand cheaper than the thing in the showroom?

What's more, because the prices of new machines are depressed, second-hand prices are being held down too, so older used bikes can be picked up relatively cheaply.

The easy way to purchase second-hand is to walk into a showroom, strike a deal and ride away. Although you may be paying up to £1000 more than if you'd bought privately, this option has obvious advantages, including:

- It's relatively hassle-free.
- The dealer might provide a loan bike while yours is being serviced.
- You can arrange finance if necessary.
- You dealer may give a warranty.
- The dealer may be willing to take in your old bike in part-exchange.
- Dealers are usually open to some haggling.
- You'll have some come-back if the bike isn't all it's cracked up to be.

However, you can usually strike a harder bargain in a private sale. If you arrive with a wad of notes in your hand, you'll be in a strong position to force the price down. The main drawback is that if the old owner has sold you a dog, getting your money back will be nigh-on impossible – so you need to know what you're doing.

Check It Out!

Whether buying privately or from a dealer, you should give a second-hand bike a thorough check-over before you come to a deal. If you don't feel confident in your mechanical ability, there is an organisation called the National Motorcycle Inspections (tel: 07050 250750) that will do the job for you.

As a rule of thumb, you should always ask to see the service history. In addition, check that the engine and frame numbers tally with the registration documents. Inspect the embossed numbers on the engine case and frame closely to make sure the originals haven't been ground away and new ones stamped. If possible, contact the previous owner (if there is one) to verify the bike's history. RiDE magazine (tel: 01733 465692) contains a detailed monthly Buyer's Guide. Purchase a copy covering the bike you're interested in, which will tell you most of what you need to know.

The main points on any used bike to look for are:
- The overall condition. If the machine is immaculate or very clean, the chances are it has been well maintained.
- Tyre wear. A new set of tyres can set you back over £250.
- Chain and rear sprocket. If the chain tensioner is nearly fully-extended, you will shortly have to part with over £100 for a new chain.
- Brake calipers and discs. The pads should have plenty of meat and shouldn't bind when you release them, while scored discs will need replacing (and you're talking about nearly £100 per front rotor).
- Headstock bearings. Move the bars from side to side to see if there's any bearing wear.
- Rear wheel bearings. Place the bike on its centre stand, or a paddock stand, and rock the wheel to see if there's play in the bearings.
- Exhaust pipes. Check these for rust. Also, if a race silencer has been fitted, you'll need the original to get through the MoT (race silencers are illegal on the road, anyway).
- Forks. Look for any oil seepage through the seals, and make sure the damping adjusters turn (they are prone to seizing).
- If any of the bolts has been drilled (such as the oil drain plug) this means that the bike has been raced.
- If the speedo is kph or the face non-standard, the bike is a parallel import.
- If the fairing has been repainted, the bike may have been crashed.

Of course, the more you find that's iffy or wrong with the bike, the more you should push the price down. Second-hand parallels don't fetch as much as official imports, and standard bikes tend to sell for more than tarted-up machines. Whatever you do, don't just buy the first machine you see. There are thousands more out there for sale, so take your time.

Chapter 4: Dressing Up For Summer

4
Dressing Up For Summer

"What's the right summer gear to wear on a bike? I see people riding in light clothing, but this makes me nervous. What happens to them if they crash? There are so many makes of leathers, boots, gloves and helmets I wouldn't know which to buy. And does money reflect quality?"
Andy, 37 years.

It's hot. The law says you have to wear a helmet, so you do. You're dressed in jeans or maybe shorts, a T-shirt or perhaps a light anorak. You go out for a spin. The feeling is exhilarating. You crash. You end up in hospital. You go through repeated operations for skin grafts and you've lost chunks of muscle. You also have to undergo blood transfusions, because of a bone infection. You leave hospital a mess, simply because you haven't worn the correct gear. And your other half is furious with you. Here's how not to become another statistic.

Why You Need Protective Gear

You need to look after your body. It was not designed to be hurled from a motorcycle at high speed without protection, land on an extremely hard, abrasive surface and then bounce, roll, slide and hit other objects. When you fall, even at slow speed, your body has to get rid of kinetic energy (the energy of motion), so your skin, muscles, nerves and bones abrade, burn and tear. Basically, you're ripped to shreds.

At 60mph (that's 88 feet per second) jeans burst open within two to four feet of sliding, or in 1/20th of a second. A light anorak provides even less protection. Trainers are completely useless, offering neither ankle nor foot protection. And your hands? They are controlled by a myriad of delicate nerve fibres supplying some 40 individual muscles in your arm, and are attached to about 30 bones via tendons, so it's folly to leave them exposed.

Although there is a European standard for manufacturing helmets, leathers and body armour, there's nothing yet to govern boots and gloves. We live in a world where profit is preferable to people, so your well-being as a born-again biker is compromised. Despite the regulations on leathers, many leather manufacturers get round them by not issuing their suits with CE Kitemarks, and then claiming they are simply fashion garments.

However, it is vital to be as well-dressed as possible. A set of leathers, boots and gloves will not always prevent injuries such as fractures, but they will reduce their number, nature and severity. Ask any racer who's walked away from a 100mph get-off.

Helmets

Buying a skid lid is a big choice. Perhaps even bigger than buying your bike. You can replace your bike, but not your brains. Our hair, scalp and skull actually do a pretty good job of protecting the brain, but in evolutionary terms the motorcycle has only been around for a fraction of a second, and homo motorcylcus' head has not yet evolved to deal with high-speed accidents.

Your grey matter, which is contained in a kind of watery sack, has all the resilience of a wet fish, so if you bang your head hard it bounces around inside the skull, which can distort and bruise it. If the bang to the head is severe (or above 400g's) the brain injures itself with the crushing effects of its own weight and you may well die.

To put this in perspective, such a blow can be delivered by walking into the edge of a door or tripping and hitting your head on pavement kerbing. A 12mph blow can deliver a 1000g rate of deceleration. Unlike other parts of the body, the brain cannot rebuild itself. That's why bonce-potties make sense.

A helmet consists of a hard outer shell that spreads impact, deflects blows and resists penetration, and a softer inner shell, a thick lining of expanded polystyrene, to absorb impact forces. When a helmet is crashed, the outer shell becomes structurally flawed and the inner, energy-absorbing polystyrene compresses, so it should not be used again. Helmets sold in Britain must comply with British Standard BS Type A or B, which is shown on a Kitemark sticker on the helmet. The A-test is the more stringent of the two, but most lids now conform to this.

Dressing Up For Summer

Choosing the right lid is vital. It's important that it fits snugly and cannot be pulled off backwards when the chin strap is secured – an ill-fitting helmet can quickly become painful and may even fall off in a crash. And unless you're willing to sacrifice your face and chin, it's advisable to wear a full-face helmet instead of one with an open face.

There's a bewildering choice of outer shells, from carbon fibre, Kevlar and fibreglass to polycarbonate. Polycarbonate lids are generally lighter and cheaper than the other helmets, but they don't receive the BS A-stamp of approval. There are also numerous types of chin straps, including ones with quick-release mechanisms (QRMs), D-rings and sliding bars. QRM straps can slacken, which may go unnoticed, while the D-ring type is pulled tight every time you put on your lid.

Finally, because of the turbulence created by the motorcycle and helmet, excessive wind noise can lead to a chronic ringing noise in your ears, called tinnitus, which can become a constant, life-long companion. This means you're going deaf. It's also horribly irritating. The current safety-at-work maximum noise level is 90 decibels (dB), while many helmets register 103dB at 60mph (with a safe daily exposure of 20 minutes) and 109dB at 100mph (with a safe daily exposure of just five minutes). With riders wearing earplugs, the noise levels at 60 and 100mph are reduced to 82dB and 96dB respectively. Take note if you ride regularly or tour.

Leathers

Buying a set of leathers is like trying to negotiate a minefield. There are cheap suits which are well-made, expensive suits that are badly-stitched and burst open on impact, and other suits which are supposedly CE-marked and then claim they're simply fashion garments. You also have the choice of one or two-piece leathers, perforated suits, suits with Kevlar panels, suits with or without body armour...the choice is endless. The plain truth is that any set of leathers is better than nothing, and leathers are an essential part of your protection.

There's a certain amount of bullshit to wade through before buying your suit. First, there are CE markings for both leathers and body armour, which guarantee a basic standard of safety for those items. The trouble is some leather manufacturers fit CE-certified body armour into suits that don't qualify for a CE mark, sew in a large CE Kitemark (which relates to the body armour only) and hopefully con the buyer into believing the leathers are up to CE standard. Make sure your leathers have a CE rating.

The second thing you'll have to wade through is the marketing hype. Fashionable leathers are usually at the expensive end of the range, but may suffer from poor stitching, weak leather, incorrect tanning (so the dye can run) and faked-up double panels. Some of the more trendy suits are also difficult and expensive to repair, and are known as 'one-crash' leathers.

Finally, you have to decide whether you go for a one-piece or two-piece suit. You'll need a one-piece if you intend to go racing (and if you're thinking of doing lots of track days a one-piece is certainly advisable), as the suit is inherently stronger. However, two-piece leathers are far more convenient for road riders.

As the salesmen in bike stores generally know little about the construction of leathers, here's a what-to-look-for guide:
- Fit: The suit should feel comfortable and allow you to move freely. If you're buying during the summer, think about colder days when you may want to wear a sweatshirt.
- Seams and stitching: Any area of the suit exposed to possible impact should be treble-stitched. The impact areas are the hips and buttocks, elbows and forearms, knees and shins, shoulders. Treble stitching incorporates two rows of stitching, concealed by stitched outer leather. The suit could burst open if single-stitched at the impact sites.

- Lining: This lets the leather slide over you and stops it tearing the skin on impact. Removable linings come out for washing, but should fasten securely with zips so they don't snag when you put on and take off the suit.
- Perforations: These little holes in the leather are ideal for hot days, but the air rushing in on cold days feels like you're being pricked by a million pins.
- Panels: The fewer panels of leather used to construct a suit the better, as every stitched area is a potential weakness. Graphics should be overlaid on the main panels, not stitched-in like patchwork. Look at the suit from the inside to see if the panels are stitched-in.
- Double leather: These should be placed over impact sites.
- Zips: Two-piece suits should have a zip attaching the jacket to the trousers that runs right the way round the waist. Half-zips at the back are less secure. Other zips, such as on the cuffs, should not be placed on impact zones and should be self-locking. There should be a flap of leather protecting the skin from the zip.
- Armour: This should not be used instead of double leather panels on impact areas. Good armour will absorb some impact and may prevent small fractures, but it will not absorb enough energy to prevent big fractures. The armour should be CE marked.
- Cuffs: Each cuff should be tight enough around your wrist to prevent the sleeve riding up your arm.
- Collar: Make sure it's comfy when you're sitting on the bike and that it doesn't push the back of your helmet up when you're in a racing crouch.
- Fabric stretch panels: Used under the arms, behind the knee and between the legs, they allow you to move easily. The material should be a blend of Kevlar (for strength) and Lycra (for elasticity).
- Leather stretch panels: Usually placed above the knees and around the small of your back, they allow for added stretch.

It's worth remembering that tailor-made suits are often no more expensive than many off-the-peg leathers, and they're obviously cut to fit exactly. Look out for brands such as BKS, Branded, Crowtree, Hideout, MJK, MW and Scott.

Gloves

If buying a set of leathers is tricky, finding the right pair of summer gloves is fraught with problems. After years of stalling, the big manufacturers have made sure there's still no European regulation governing gloves.

Some of the cheaper gloves, selling for around £30, are well-made, while some gloves retailing for over £100 are rubbish. Expensive, fashionable gloves don't always offer the best protection. The dye in many makes runs when you sweat or when the leather is wet, and don't forget that the dye used in leather could be harmful.

However, your gloves should be a snug fit, allow free movement of your hands and give good feel of the bike's controls. Here's what to look for:

- Leather: There's a trade-off between safety and feel. The thicker the leather, the greater protection it will provide, but the more it will restrict movement. However, some thin leather gloves abrade in 0.6 seconds on impact, which is insufficient. Gloves with few panels will be stronger. Try on different makes before you buy.
- Abrasion protection: An extra layer of leather over the palm and wrist area is important, as you tend to land palm-side down and there are vital blood vessels and nerves in the wrist. An extra layer over the little finger and back of the hand is also a good idea.
- Kevlar: This gives useful added protection when properly used, but some gloves boast Kevlar protection and have something the size of a postage stamp sewn in.
- Metal studs: These tend to rip the leather on impact and offer little protection. They should be separated from the skin because they get hot with friction.
- Armour: Padding on the back of the hand and knuckles will reduce impact. Gloves with rounded carbon fibre knuckles should be comfortable.
- Wrist restraint: These stop the glove being pulled off. A Velcro strap that adjusts to fit is better than elasticated material.
- Lining: There shouldn't be any lining over the palm area, as it reduces feel. Thin lining on the back of the hand gives some insulation.
- Stitching: Double-row stitching is preferable to single. The main seams should be double-stitched and overlaid with leather in the

knuckle, little finger and palm area.
- Cuff: Make sure the cuff is long enough, so your wrist is not exposed when you stretch your arm. There should be a cuff strap.

Boots

Until recently summer boots were made from leather. Then Lorica became the norm. Lorica is a man-made material – a plastic – that's soft, comfy, cheap and easy to work with. But alas many riders feel that it offers all the protection of a pair of bedroom slippers. Lorica appears to abrade easily, so you might rightly ask why some boots made from this material retail for up to £200. The trouble is most of us are stuck with the stuff, because it's now hard to find leather boots. And of course there's no European standard for motorcycle boots.

Unfortunately, injuries to the lower leg are among the most common to result from bike crashes. Breaking your ankle can have serious, long-term consequences (like you might never walk properly again, or else walk with a permanent limp) and being forced (through ignorance or lack of choice) to wear a material that offers naff-all abrasion resistance is disgraceful. You may have to hunt around for a pair of leather boots, but it's well worth it.

When looking for a pair of summer boots, consider the following:
- Material: Buy leather, if possible.
- Armour: Hard shields and foam padding over the ankle area and shin can dissipate impact forces.
- Zips: These should be on the inside of the leg, away from the impact area. A three-quarter length zip with a Velcro top flap allows for different-sized calves. Boots fastened purely with a Velcro flap are liable to rip off.
- Sliders: These protect your toes at extreme lean angles. Screw-in toe sliders are more secure than Velcro ones.
- Gear-change reinforcement: Constant wear from the gear lever can damage the boot. The reinforcement should be overlaid, not stitched on.
- Sole: Race boots tend to have thinner soles than road boots, but do not absorb vibration as efficiently. The soles should flex lengthways for walking, but should be rigid sideways to protect feet from being crushed.

- Lining: Perforated leather linings are more comfortable and cooler than fabric linings.
- Heel Cup: This should be rigid for protection.

Saving Your Skin

Dr Rod Woods, of Cambridge University, has devised an abrasion test for material. Here's how long it takes different materials to hole:

Denim	0.2 to 0.5 secs
Average bike glove	1.0 to 1.8 secs
Waxed cotton (two layers)	1.3 secs
Boot leather	2.2 to 20 secs, depending on thickness
Cow hide (3mm thick)	3.8 secs
Kevlar (two layers)	5.6 secs
Two layers of cow hide	18 secs
Leather stretch panels	20.4 secs
Three layers of cow hide	55 secs

Dressing For Summer

Follow our ten tips on how to dress for summer:
1. Buy a helmet that fits. The most expensive lids may not offer greater protection than cheaper ones, but their quality of construction will be superior.
2. BS A-type lids are more stringently tested than B-marked ones.
3. Wear ear plugs when you ride. Wind noise can seriously damage your ears.
4. If possible, buy leathers that display a CE Kitemark that is applicable to the leathers.
5. The body armour in your leather suit should be CE-marked as well.
6. Your leathers should be a comfortable fit. Use the check-list when buying.
7. Use the check list when buying gloves.
8. Buy a pair of leather boots if possible and use the check list.
9. Price does not always reflect quality when buying leathers, boots and gloves.
10. Carry a fold-away, one-piece waterproof oversuit for rainy days.

Chapter 5: Wrapping Up For Winter

5
Wrapping Up For Winter

"There's no way I'm riding through the winter. It's far too cold and, anyway, I hate getting wet. Give me a comfy, well-heated car any day. As far as I'm concerned, the bike stays in the garage until the sun re-appears."
Jack, 48 years.

Most bikes owned by born-again bikers go into hibernation during the winter. And so do their owners. The latter curl up in front of the fire, watch telly, suffer motorcycle withdrawal symptoms, and dream of blossoming flowers and warm spring days. Their machines, they feel, are far too precious to see a drop of rain, but – worst of all – they themselves might get cold and wet.

Who wants to venture out in miserable weather, get their machine covered in road salt, and return home with a soaked crotch and sponge-like gloves? Worrying about your bike deteriorating through the winter is very understandable (a winter hack solves that problem). But riding in winter doesn't all have to be frozen fingers, weeping eyes and uncontrollable shivers. Motorcycling in the wet may be an acquired taste, although once you overcome the fear of slippery roads it's both a real challenge and great fun. There are also ways of cosseting yourself while tackling the elements.

Your two enemies, naturally, are the wet and the cold. While it's possible to remain toasty-warm in even the most extreme temperatures, it's far harder to stay bone dry, as anyone who's suffered leaky waterproofs will tell you.

That Creeping Agony – The Cold

The first thing that happens when you start to get cold is that your hands and feet begin to go numb. As your body continues to lose heat your extremities become ever more painful, your fingers seize up and your arms and legs become rigid. Eventually you suffer hypothermia, your concentration wanders, you have difficulty controlling the bike, and by now you wish you weren't on the damned thing anyway. It's a miserable, nasty experience – and quite avoidable.

Most people's reaction is to fit heated handlebar grips, or wear heated gloves. Well, if your hands get cold, you need to keep them warm, don't you? That logic, however, is faulty because the secret lies in maintaining your core temperature. Your extremities become cold first because, as your main body temperature drops, the blood supply to the outer areas is automatically reduced. If your body's core temperature drops by just two degrees, you can go into hypothermia. Conversely, your hands and feet can still operate when their temperature has dropped to as low as 15°C. Crucially, by keeping your core temperature up, your hands and feet will remain warmer.

The bitter cold can catch people out too. The temperature may not feel that low when you wander out of your nice, warm home, simply because you're toasty and you haven't taken the wind chill factor into account. For every six mph increase in speed, the temperature drops by 1°C. What appears like a relatively mild day can suddenly turn freezing cold once you get moving.

Everyone who rides through the winter works out their own method of staying warm. My perception of winter riding changed forever when I discovered the electrically-heated jacket, which included heated sleeves and a heated collar. Since using this simple device I've thoroughly enjoyed year-round biking and, with the exception of touring Norway in temperatures reaching minus 20°C, I've never been cold. Other people resort to layers of thermals, while some are happy with heated grips and gloves.

Heated Kit

Electrically-heated gear is now widely available. It's an excellent method of staying warm, because it both retains and generates heat. There's a wide selection to choose from, including gloves, handlebar grips, inner soles and trousers.

However, because you want to maintain a good core temperature, your best bet is to go for an electrically-heated jacket. If you buy a heated jacket that includes heated arms and collar, you won't need other heated gear. What's more, you won't need layer upon layer of thermals.

Here's what to look for when buying a heated jacket:
- Make sure the jacket's voltage matches that of the bike, as most jackets run off 12-volt systems.
- It should be fuse-protected.
- Temperature control is useful, because your body temperature will fluctuate as the bike's speed changes.
- Ensure that the electrical lead is long enough for you to sit on the bike comfortably.
- Easy-to-understand instructions should come with it. In most cases an electrical lead is attached to the bike's battery terminals and the jacket's lead plugs into that.

Thermals

Thermals come in all shapes, sizes and thicknesses: fleece jackets, polo necks, long-sleeved shirts, T-shirts, leggings, socks, gloves, balaclavas and neck warmers. Layers are the name of the thermal game, but of course once you're dressed up and inside a winter suit, it's difficult to control your temperature without stripping off and re-layering yourself.

Good thermals, however, will wick away sweat from your body and they are fairly efficient at retaining warmth. Experience will tell you how many layers you require, but make sure they don't restrict body movement too much and that you're able to have a pee (there's nothing more frustrating than fumbling around with fingers stiff with cold).

Balaclavas and neck warmers are essential wear (even with a heated jacket) as there's a massive heat loss through the head and neck. Make sure the back of the neck is well covered and that the material fits snugly into the collar of your jacket, as otherwise you'll find uncomfortable draughts whistling through in no time.

Outer Layers

I always recommend wearing leathers, but once you start adding serious winter gear as well (heated jacket, thermals and an oversuit) you quickly metamorphose into an immobile blob. You won't be able to bend your arms and legs easily and you'll probably be horribly uncomfortable on the bike.

Many winter oversuits now have body armour and are made of reasonably abrasion-resistant material. One-piece oversuits are best at retaining heat, while two-piece suits are generally more useful. If you opt for a two-piece suit, make sure there's a good overlap between the jacket and trousers to exclude draughts.

Here's what to look for when buying a winter oversuit:
- The outer material should be mostly Cordura (a synthetic material with good tear resistance). Nylon is cheaper and not so hard-wearing.
- There should be a waterproof liner. Although the outer fabric will fend off some water, you need an inner lining to beat off the rest. Names such as Gore-Tex, Sympatex and Porelle are a good bet.
- Make sure there's a thermal inner lining. Removable thermal linings increase a jacket's versatility, as the jacket can be worn year-round.

- It should contain CE-marked body armour on the shoulders, elbows, hips and knees. Some jackets include back protectors.
- The inside of the collar should be made of soft material and the collar should be easily adjustable. Try the jacket on while wearing a helmet, to make sure the collar doesn't catch or prevent you moving your head.
- The cuffs should wrap up so your gloves will go over them, and open wide enough to tuck winter gloves inside (as water can run down the sleeves of the jacket and into the gloves, especially while riding sports bikes).
- The bottom of the trousers should fit over your boots and secure simply and quickly.
- Zips should be accessible to gloved hands and the main body zip must have an underflap to keep water out.
- There should be at least one inner pocket that will always remain dry (outer pockets invariably leak).
- Seams in vulnerable areas should have at least one row of concealed stitching for abrasion resistance. All seams should be taped on the inside.
- The main zip of a one-piece suit should extend from the neck to half way down the thigh, making it easy to get in and out of the suit.

Winter Boots

Now you've worked out how to keep your core temperature up, there's no need for your feet to suffer. However, you'll still need a pair of winter boots, which vary from lined leather boots to clod-hopping motocross boots. Good-quality winter boots will not leak.

Here's what to look for:
- Buy boots that are slightly too big for you. You'll want to insert thermal inner soles and wear thick socks in really cold weather.
- The outer material of the boot should be made of leather.
- Look for waterproof linings with the Gore-Tex, Porelle and Sympatex brand names.
- Make sure the boots are tall enough to be covered by your waterproof trousers when you're sitting on the bike.
- Armour around the shins and ankles helps absorb impacts.

- Rigid, pre-formed heel and toe cups provide added protection.
- The soles should flex lengthways, but be rigid sideways, so your feet don't get crushed in an accident.
- The gear-change pad should be overlaid and not stitched into the boot. The pad is to prevent wear on the outer material.
- A fabric gusset with a waterproof membrane will hold back the water that leaks past the zip.

Winter Gloves

Gloves are a perennial headache because so many brands leak in downpours. And even if the gloves don't leak, water can easily seep in past the cuffs. However, a good pair should remain water-resistant for at least one winter and offer decent protection in a spill.

When buying winter gloves, make sure you choose a size that allows room for thermal inner gloves. The outer material should be leather at least 1mm thick, with double leather across the palms for abrasion resistance. Man-made materials like Cordura or nylon aren't so abrasion-resistant and should have leather overlays on vulnerable areas. Brand names such as Thinsulate, Thermolite, Thermotex and Trispace offer good insulation. Some gloves have foil liners to reduce heat loss.

Winter gloves should have a waterproof inner liner between the outer material and the thermal lining. It's usually a plastic membrane, with millions of micro-pores, that claims to repel rain yet allow sweat to escape, although the waterproofing tends to fail first at high-pressure points (the area where you squeeze the levers). And there should be wrist straps to keep the gloves on in a crash and to keep draughts out. A Velcro adjustment is best. To test, put the glove on, tighten the wrist strap, and try to pull the glove off. Look for stretch panels on the knuckles and joints which allow easy hand movement, although a well-designed glove might not need them. The cuff should be long enough to prevent gaps between the glove and sleeve of your jacket.

The thermal lining shouldn't be stitched in (as this causes leaks), but it shouldn't pull out either. Try the glove on several times to make sure the lining doesn't bunch up.

But That's Not All...

Winter riding also requires some additional bits and pieces:
- A misty visor is a pain in the butt, as it dangerously reduces visibility. In extreme cold the inside of your visor can ice up, which means you'll have to ride with your visor open. There are various demisting sprays and liquids that prevent misting for a short while, but fitting a Fog City visor liner is the only way to completely prevent misting and icing. The Fog City liner adheres to the inside of the visor and acts like double glazing.
- You may wish to carry a specialist visor cleaning kit with you, which conventionally comprises of a bottle of cleaning fluid, with an attached sponge and wiper.
- If you spurn street cred and love warm, dry hands, consider handlebar muffs. They fit over the handlebars and your hands fit inside to operate the levers. Because they are made of relatively soft material, they can compress against the brake and clutch levers at speed.

Winter Woollies

My ultimate winter wardrobe consists of the following:
1. Thermal leggings
2. Thermal socks

3. Thermal polo neck
4. Thermal balaclava
5. Thermal inner gloves
6. Electrically-heated jacket
7. Salopettes
8. Winter jacket
9. Winter gloves
10. Winter boots

Chapter 6: The Law & Insurance

6
The Law & Insurance

"I got stopped for speeding, but I was hardly going fast. When the traffic cop looked at the bike, it was obvious he wasn't going to caution me. He picked out my black visor and my race silencer immediately – and threw the book at me. All right, I was a bit abusive too."
Mark, 48 years.

Living with a motorcycle usually involves flirting with the law. Black visors, loud exhaust pipes, small number plates and tinted headlamp covers are common enough accessories, but they are all illegal. And let's face it, unless you've bought a custom bike, you're hardly likely to stick to 60mph down your favourite section of country road. So how far dare you push the envelope? Here are a few words of advice.

PART ONE – THE LAW

Riding Style

Good riding is largely about being sensible. Many traffic cops own bikes and are perfectly happy to speed themselves – if the conditions are right. Speeding in itself is not inherently dangerous; what matters is where and how you choose to do it. If you're caught speeding, but are riding responsibly, you may well get away with a caution. If you're recklessly hooning around, without a care in the world, you'll almost certainly be nicked.

However, the rise in solo motorcycle accidents and country road fatalities means the police in certain counties are becoming increasingly bullish in their attitude towards born-again bikers. Fed up with scraping bodies off their roads, they are turning from education to direct enforcement and, with the connivance of the magistrates, are going for the maximum penalties. All those go-faster goodies you stick on your bike will only attract extra attention from the boys in blue.

However, a RiDE magazine survey of traffic cops around the country showed that the responsible rider is far more likely to be cautioned than the reckless rider. Here are the results:

race exhaust
Responsible rider: 70% stop rider for a word, 30% caution.
Reckless rider: 100% caution/book rider.

black visor
Responsible rider: 50% stop rider for a word, 40% caution, 10% ignore.
Reckless rider: 50% caution, 40% book, 10% ignore.

undersized numberplate
Responsible rider: 50% caution, 40% stop rider for a word, 10% ignore.
Reckless rider: 80% book, 20% caution.

tinted headlight cover
Responsible rider: 60% stop rider for a word, 40% caution.
Reckless rider: 70% caution, but 100% will book for a red or blue cover.

bad or unsafe riding
Responsible rider: 100% stop rider for a word.
Reckless rider: 60% caution, 40% stop rider for a word.

racing on the road
Responsible rider: 80% book, 20% caution.
Reckless rider: 100% book.

knee down/wheelie
Responsible rider: 60% stop rider for a word, 20% caution, 20% ignore.
Reckless rider: 70% book, 30% caution.

Sensible Attitude

But that's not the end of the story. When you do get pulled for speeding on your tarted-up race replica with its horribly noisy pipe, how you confront the policeman will also make a difference. However hard it may seem at the time, however discriminated against you may feel, treat the kindly copper like a human being. For your own good, take the following precautionary steps:
1. Stop the engine, get off the bike and remove your helmet.
2. Behave politely. It can make the difference between being cautioned or being given a ticket.

Back In The Saddle

3. Don't grovel either.
4. If you can, produce your driving licence, and insurance and registration papers.

Warning: Being nice to cops may have no effect, so after the b@st*rd has booked you anyway and is out of sight and sound, use any expletive you wish!

Think and Plan

How you ride constitutes a big part of the equation. If you're going brains-out and you're too engrossed to notice the jam sandwich, or the police motorcyclist in the lay-by dolled up in dayglo yellow, what else will you miss?

You should always ride well within your limits. That means giving your eyes the opportunity of 360-degree observation and your cerebral mass some chance of taking it all in. Your brain needs time to process the mass of information from ahead (mainly), your periphery (importantly) and from behind (with the help of your mirrors).

Put yourself in the position of the police and think where speed traps or police cars may be positioned. The obvious places are where the road opens up and encourages you to speed, in roadside cuttings, on bridges (especially over motorways) where they can see you a mile off, behind hedgerows, or between slow-moving lorries.

Urban 'orrors

Speeding in most city centres is not a big issue – if only because the traffic is so dense. But there are areas in any town where it's possible to speed, and you won't get far these days without being caught. Here's what you're up against:

<u>Unmarked police cars</u>
These look like spotlessly-clean, bog-standard motors, but have hidden extras like blue flashing lights hidden behind the grille, twin interior rear view mirrors, possibly a VASCAR on the dashboard, a flip-up stop sign (about the size of a video recorder) on the parcel shelf, two or more aerials and it will be devoid of dealer stickers. It will be driven by a smart man wearing a white shirt with shoulder lapels and a black tie. His passenger (if he has one) will be similarly dressed.

<u>Gatso speed cameras</u>
These are large, grey boxes mounted on a grey, square-section post and there will be thin white markers painted on the road nearby. Roadside warning signs will warn you of their presence. If the box is live, it will flash twice to record your speed; if it flashes once it doesn't contain any film (only one in eight Gatsos contain film). If the camera does record you speeding, you will receive a fixed penalty within 14 days or an invitation to court, but if the paperwork drops through your letterbox after 14 days, it's no longer valid.

<u>Forward-facing cameras</u>
These look like Gatsos, but have red lenses. As they only photograph oncoming traffic, they are not a problem for bikers (neither are similarly set-up Gatsos).

VASCAR

This is a box situated on the dashboard of a police car that calculates your speed over a given distance. It can either be used in pursuit between two fixed points (white road markers or bridges, for example) or, once it has calculated the given distance, Mr Plod can hide in a lay-by and time your average speed.

Hand-held speed guns

These are mostly used in towns and villages, but are also sometimes used in the countryside. Some police wear yellow jackets and stand proudly by the edge of the road, making it quite obvious they're manning a speed trap, but others will hide behind cars, bridge supports or hedges and pop out when they've caught you.

Motorway Madness

Motorways are a joy to car drivers. To bikers they are boring, boring, interminably boring. Before you know it you've wandered off into a world of dreams, itches start appearing where they can't be reached...and suddenly, without realising it, you're cruising at 100mph. If that's the way you ride you'll soon be taking the bus. The trouble is, the police love motorways too. Here's how to hedge your bets and stay awake:

- forward vision. Use plenty of it, always scan the road well ahead in order to plan your next move.
- mirrors. Use them constantly to see what cars are approaching from behind. Mirrors are a lifesaver anyway.
- passing cars. Check out the cars you overtake, treating each one as an unmarked police car.
- following cars. Be wary of cars approaching you from behind. If you think an unmarked car might be following you, slow down and let it pass.
- faster car. If you wish to speed up, wait for a car to overtake you, check it out to see if it's an unmarked police car, and then follow it at a distance, using it as a second pair of eyes. If there's a speed trap ahead, the police will hopefully spot the car before they clock you.
- bridges. Check out every bridge. The police stand or park on bridges, as they give a clear view down the motorway. A car parked on a bridge may belong to a sales rep on his mobile, but could just as easily belong to the Plod.

- speed markers. White squares painted on the motorway are used to measure your speed between two points. Make sure you're not being followed or that there are no police up ahead.
- service stations. A favoured police haunt. Scan service stations as you ride past and keep an eye in your mirrors as you pass slip roads.
- road works: With increasing frequency nowadays, long stretches of road works have a reduced speed limit, monitored by speed traps.

Country Capers

Swooping, undulating, twisty country roads are a biker's dream, but they can easily suck you into scratching mode, where you're more worried about the next bend than that funny man with the yellow jacket you saw lurking behind a tree.

Here are things to look out for when driving in the countryside (apart from Gatsos, white speed markings and hidden traffic cars):

- urban areas. No, it's not clever to speed through towns or villages. It's not safe and it's extremely anti-social.
- solid white lines. Overtake on solid white lines and you won't be Mr Plod's flavour of the month, even if the manoeuvre is safe. If you are going to cross a double white line, make sure you're not about to overtake a cop car too.
- biker spots. Biker haunts attract police like flies to...so beware. They are cops' favoured spots for purging our green and pleasant land of undersized number plates, race silencers, tinted headlamp covers and general biker scum. It's the one place where you can rest assured the cops will not be friendly. Only doing me job, mate!

PART TWO – INSURANCE

Look Around

The law requires you to have adequate insurance when you take your bike on the road. But although born-again bikers often have the advantage of age when it comes to insurance premium calculations, it doesn't always work out that way.

The horrible truth is that, unless you're a reasonably experienced, sensible biker, you might not be able to insure the machine of your dreams. You may be able to afford the bike itself, but you could have real difficulty finding insurance cover for it. When it comes to machines like the Yamaha R1, Honda FireBlade, Kawasaki ZX-9R and Suzuki's Hayabusa, insurance companies are avoiding born-agains like the plague.

> I'M SORRY, MR SPIKE, BUT WE ONLY INSURE RESPONSIBLE ADULTS

Even if you do get cover for these machines, the company will stipulate that the insurance is only valid if the bike is garaged at home, and if it is fitted with an approved alarm and immobiliser system. The insurance company will ask for proof of a two- or three-year no claims bonus as well.

So before you even walk into the showrooms, obtain quotes from several different insurers. The first thing you'll find is that some companies will offer cover while others won't, and that the premiums and conditions on offer will vary wildly from company to company. This is because each insurer bases your premium on its experience of riders with your profile, and because some brokers secure cheaper policies with insurance companies than others.

While you're on the phone, give the broker the details asked for and prompt for some form of discount. You may have taken an advanced riding course, or cover a limited mileage, or may be willing to pay a higher excess (the amount you have to cough up when you make a claim). If you've been offered lower quotes than the one on offer, say so, and if you haven't make up a believable figure and throw that in.

It's also worth contacting the bike manufacturers' brokers. Honda, Kawasaki, Yamaha, Suzuki, Ducati and BMW all have insurance schemes for owners. While these may not always be the cheapest, they usually offer fringe benefits like reduced spares prices and track day cover. However, if you are buying a new bike, check out the premium you're likely to be offered in your second year, as some premiums rocket after the first year.

Making It Cheaper

Here are some ways of reducing your premium, without sacrificing the quality of insurance cover:

Get Trained Up

Insurance companies like riders who have taken an advanced course, such as those offered by the IAM, Rospa and qualified police instructors. They reckon that people who receive such training are less likely to stuff their bikes into hedges. You may have to produce a certificate as proof of training. As your chances of having an accident after training are reduced, you're more likely to build up a four or five-year no-claims bonus, which could drop your premium by up to 50 per cent.

Think About Your Job

Your job may be no more than a weekly grind to you, but to the insurer it's an important way of pegging your premium. The logic is that the riskier your job, the more likely you are to take risks, so telling the insurance company that you're a bomb disposal expert won't go down well. In addition, if you are in the media, or are a professional sportsperson or a celeb, you'll be hit hard because you may well carry some mega-wealthy star as pillion. Insurance companies may have different perceptions about what constitutes a high-risk job, so keep ringing round if you're experiencing problems. You'll also be asked whether your bike will be used for work. Commuting isn't considered work use, and if you never commute on your bike the premium may be reduced again.

You Need A Garage

Some insurance companies will not offer a quote unless you have a garage at home. Others will offer a discount even if the bike's going to be housed in a garden shed, or if you use a mate's garage down the road. However, if you are bereft of a garage, an alarm/immobiliser and locks could help bring that premium down.

Don't Claim

So you've crashed your bike and scuffed the fairing. To replace the parts will cost £500, but your excess is £400. Don't claim without serious thought, as your no-claims discount could vanish in a puff of smoke and your premium may be increased the following year. In addition, there are firms which will repair minor damage, such as scuffed fairings, more cheaply than the cost of new parts.

The Small Print...

Don't just rush in when you're offered the lowest quote – read the small print. A low quote may contain hidden clauses that you'll only find out about when you make a claim. When you're making enquiries, disclose all your information to the broker, make sure you know the excess involved, and check for limits to claims and annual mileages. Also, ask what extras accompany the policy, as you may decide you don't need them all. And if you are taking out TPFT (third party, fire and theft) make sure you can upgrade to comprehensive if necessary.

Ten Top Tips On How To Beat The Old Bill

1. If you're going to speed, use your head. Think about the advice given earlier in this chapter.
2. You're best off on a bog-standard bike. Go-faster goodies only attract unwanted attention.

3. Always have adequate and up-to-date insurance cover for your bike whenever it's on the road.
4. You should never ride so fast that you miss seeing the police – or other hazards for that matter.
5. Take your driving licence with you when you are out on a ride, as this will answer some of the questions the traffic cop might have.
6. Ride responsibly, showing consideration for other road users. Don't be selfish or reckless.
7. Think like a copper; ask yourself where speed traps might be hidden and adjust your riding accordingly.
8. Get some advanced training. It will reduce your chance of having an accident – you might even be told how to look out for traffic cops!
9. If you are stopped by the police, be polite and respectful. It can't do you any harm..
10. Only effing-bleedin-bloody swear at the police when they're out of earshot – then you can curse at them as much as you want.

Chapter 7: Where You Can Go

7
Where You Can Go

"After I bought my bike, I realised that I was on my own. None of my friends are into motorcycles, so I ride on my tod, which is a bit boring. I'd really like to meet some like-minded people, so I could have a laugh and go out for the occasional thrash together."
Alan, 35 years.

You've just returned to motorcycling and have bought the bike of your dreams. You take it out for its first spin. It's fast, so much faster than anything you owned in the past. And boy, does it handle! Your eyes are out on stalks, you return home buzzing. You walk through the front door, grinning from ear to ear - and you want to tell the world about it. But your partner isn't interested, and neither are your friends. It's one huge disappointment.

The harsh truth is that many people buy a motorcycle and then discover they have no playmates. But bikers are gregarious. They like to swap stories, fantasise, see hundreds of other bikes and discuss the merits of their machines. That's why there are so many meeting places throughout Britain, and one reason why race events are so popular.

But if you decide to join the weekend meeting-place deluge, don't forget about Mr Plod. He and his friends will almost certainly be there too, ready to nick you for speeding, or not having a tax disc, or wearing a black visor, or for fitting a race exhaust to your bike, or... Here are some of the main biking events in the born-again's diary:

Boxhill, Dorking, Surrey
Established in the swinging 60s, Boxhill is the haunt of hundreds. Every Sunday bikers gather to show off, ogle metal and have a good chin-wag. There's a café for grub and a cuppa - and a heavy police presence.
<u>Venue</u>: North of Dorking on the A24.

High Beech, Epping Forest, east London
Steeped in biking history. High Beech hosted the first British speedway race in 1923 – although you'd never know by visiting the place now. It's sedate, with bikers pulling up for a chat and a cuppa.
Venue: A112, south of junction 26 of the M25.

Chelsea Bridge
Chelsea's the spot, innit? Yeah, you can watch nutters wheelie and then scarper before the Old Bill scream onto the scene. It's a Saturday night event and offers the usual cuppa, and a blast along the A4 to the Heston services on the M4 near Heathrow.
Venue: Chelsea Bridge, Chelsea, London, near A4.

Stratford-upon-Avon Waterfront
Ride down to the waterfront and you'll be greeted by a special area earmarked for bikers only. Stratford has the usual town amenities and some good places to eat.
Venue: Waterfront, Stratford-upon-Avon, Warks.

North Parade, Matlock Bath, Derbyshire
Ride into Matlock over the weekend and you'll be greeted by the sight of hundreds of bikes parked along the side of the road. You'll find all types of machines here, from customs to sportsters. It's a rider's Mecca, with a host of fantastic twisties within easy reach. But it's well policed – as are the surrounding roads, especially the Cat and Fiddle run.
Venue: Matlock Bath, on the A6 north of Derby.

Devil's Bridge, Kirkby Longsdale, Cumbria
Another biker venue surrounded by twisty roads. Turn up any Sunday, take in the atmosphere and sample the yummee delights of the Chuck Wagon. You may also get the chance to watch loonies jump off the bridge and plummet 40 feet into the River Lune.
Venue: On the A65, south-east of junction 36 of the M6.

Squire's Coffee Bar, Sherburn-in-Elmet, Yorkshire
A biker-friendly café offering a warm welcome. There's a juke box, lots of leather-clad folk, and it's best on a Sunday.
Venue: Close to Castleford and Tadcaster, on the A162 in North Yorkshire.

Kent Custom Show

The meeting place for custom bike fans. The Hell's Angels, who run the show, police the event. While it isn't a typical family day out, a wide range of bikers attend. The show has competitions for best custom bike or chopper, and there's a huge array of stalls and bars. At night rock bands entertain the crowds. The Show is held early summer.
Venue: County Showground, near Maidstone, Kent. Call 01634 270189.

YOU CAN GO TO THE KENT CUSTOM SHOW...

Bull Dog Bash, Avon Park, Stratford-upon-Avon, Warwickshire

Avon Park is a drag strip and during the rally you'll have the chance to flip your bike when the lights go green, or better still race your mate down the eighth-of-a-mile strip. That's the central attraction and it's watched by thousands. Away from the drag strip there are tattoo parlours, stalls, food and bars, plus the most amazing collection of bikes and bikers. Avon Park is at Long Marston Airfield, halfway between Stratford-upon-Avon and Broadway on the B4632. The Bash is held at the beginning of August, usually over a Bank Holiday weekend.
For more info call 01634 270189.

BMF Rally, The Showground, Peterborough

The Rally is usually held at the beginning of May, at the East of England Showground in Peterborough. The Showground is near Alwalton, just south-west of Peterborough, and bang on the A1. The Rally attracts around 100,000 people, making it the biggest show in Britain, and it kicks off the biking calendar. The show includes manufacturers' bike displays, mad moped endurance racing, a mass of stalls selling everything you can think of, stunt riding and long-jump competitions, the Wall of Death and other attractions. The jamboree lasts three days, but the first two days are open to BMF members only. The last day is open to the public.

<u>Venue</u>: Peterborough. Call the BMF for details on 0181 949 6215.

...YOU CAN JOIN THE BMF RIDE-IN...

The Motorcycle Show, NEC

Your chance to see the latest on offer. All the new bikes will be there, plus hundreds of firms in the trade – this is where you'll find all the big names in the industry. The Bike Show is also a sprawling motorcycling supermarket, where you can buy anything from kiddies' leathers to anodised bolts. The show, which runs for over a week, is packed solid at the weekend and a little less solidly during the week. Be prepared to do some barging. There is a free, secure bike park and somewhere to leave your helmet in safety.

<u>Venue</u>: National Exhibition Centre, off the M42, near Birmingham. Call 01203 251515 for info and tickets.

The Isle of Man TT

The TT used to be the greatest event in the international racing calendar. Although it no longer attracts the best road racers in the world, it's still a sight to behold. Watching competitors race between stone walls and thick hedgerows is breathtaking – and the event continues to be a wonderful biking festival. The TT lasts two weeks and traditionally takes place over the last week of May and the first week of June. The first week is dedicated to practice and the second week is when the racing takes place. During race week the Island is awash with bikers. During the day you can watch the racing from vantage points along the thirty-seven-and-a-quarter mile course, while in the evenings you can get pissed as a rat (although a few people manage to remain remarkably sober). Douglas boasts such notable events as the Miss Wet T-Shirt Competition, rock bands and impromptu burn-outs along its promenade. There are also stunt shows, ride-outs and mini-moto racing. The first Sunday of the race week is when Mad Sunday happens, where the 10 miles of the circuit between Creg-ny-baa and Ramsey Hairpin becomes a one-way race track, and where speed limits apply in the villages only. But be warned that there's a good splattering of nutters out on the road – and some of them do get splattered. It's safest to ride out early morning or early evening. Accommodation on the Island can range from classy hotels to tent sites, but you must book well in advance. The ferry crossing to the Island is not cheap, and that should be booked early in the year too. The Island's plain-clothes police look like something out of a bad black-and-white B-movie, and they and their sniffer dogs await all wandering ashore, so be warned.

Useful numbers:
Tourist info (for accommodation details): 01624 686766.
Isle of Man Steam Packet ferries: 01624 661661.

British Superbike Championship

The premier racing class in Britain is considered one of the best in the world. It's based on production motorcycles that can be bought from dealers, but the bikes are heavily modified. The racing is usually very close and there are a host of support races as well. Each Superbike race comprises two legs and the meetings are held at the major tracks in Britain, including: Donington Park (eight miles south east of Derby; 01332 810048), Brands Hatch (off the M20, 20 miles south east of London; 01474 872331), Silverstone (A43 between Towcester and Brackley,

Northants; 01327 857271), Cadwell Park (off the A153 between Horncastle and Louth, in Lines; 01507 343248), Knockhill (A823 five miles south of Dumfermline, Fife; 01383 723337), Mallory Park (A47 between Hinckley and Leicester; 01455 842931), Oulton Park (A54 near Tarporley, Cheshire; 01829 760301), Thruxton (A303, two miles west of Andover; 01264 772607), Snetterton (All between Thetford and Attleborough, Norfolk; 01953 887303).

World Superbike, Donington Park and Brands Hatch
The World Superbike circus descends on Donington Park, near Derby, in April and offers you the chance to see the world's best four-stroke riders scrap it out in some hair-raising battles. After a bit of globetrotting, the series returns to Britain in August, usually over the last Bank Holiday weekend, where huge crowds flock to Brands Hatch circuit, near Fawkham in Kent. If you want to witness elbow-to-elbow scraps, the WSB series is the place to be. And Brands is a superb spectator circuit with great views.

British Grand Prix, Donington Park
This is where you can see motorcycling's gods wrestle with the most advanced two-wheeled technology available. Unfortunately us Brits spend our money watching the World Superbikes and we don't seem to give a damn about the GPs. Mind you, Donington Park is not a good spectator circuit – and there isn't a Brit among the front-runners. The 125, 250 and 500 classes are still an awesome sight, and there's still some fairing-bashing racing, especially in the two smaller classes. The British GP is usually held in July, at Donington Park, near Derby.

North West 200, Coleraine, Londonderry, Northern Ireland
This is the warm-up to the Isle of Man TT and takes place during May. Everything from 125s to superbikes race along the roads between Coleraine, Portstewart and Portrush. The majority of spectating is free around the course (and you get very close to the action), although entry to the grandstand will cost. There are lots of relatively cheap and pleasant bed-and-breakfast establishments in each of the three towns and every centre has a helpful tourist office, which will give you accommodation contacts.

Skerries, near Dublin, Ireland

If you think the TT is hairy, then go to Skerries. This is the place where racers leave their brains safely tucked up in their tool boxes and then go bananas down narrow, bumpy, Irish country roads. Definitely the maddest event of all. There are no gravel traps or tyre walls, just the odd straw bale and lots of nasty-looking hedges, grass banks and trees – and you can dangle your legs inches from the bikes as they fly by. But Skerries is also a big party, hosted by the most hospitable people in the world. It attracts crowd sizes to shame British racing and traditionally takes place at the beginning of July.

...OR YOU CAN EVEN SPECTATE AT SKERRIES!

Le Mans, Le Mans circuit, northern France

Le Mans kicks off the gruelling, 24-hour endurance race series. There is invariably some British interest, with several of our racers taking part. The event usually takes place mid-April. The town of Le Mans is only four hours ride from Calais. Racing starts at 3pm Saturday and finishes 3pm Sunday. A ticket will give you a place to pitch your tent and a grandstand seat.

Assen World Superbikes, Circuit van Drenthe, Assen, Holland

When the Dutch have a race meeting, they turn it into a party. Assen becomes a biker's heaven, which is why there's an annual pilgrimage of Brits to the place. But the fast, flowing circuit offers you the chance to witness some of the best racing in the world - it's also an excellent spectator track. Assen is easiest reached by taking the ferry to the Hook of Holland, which saves you the long, boring slog along the motorways from Calais. The Circuit van Drenthe is on the A28 Groningen road, just south west of Assen.

Chapter 8: Touring The Great Unknown

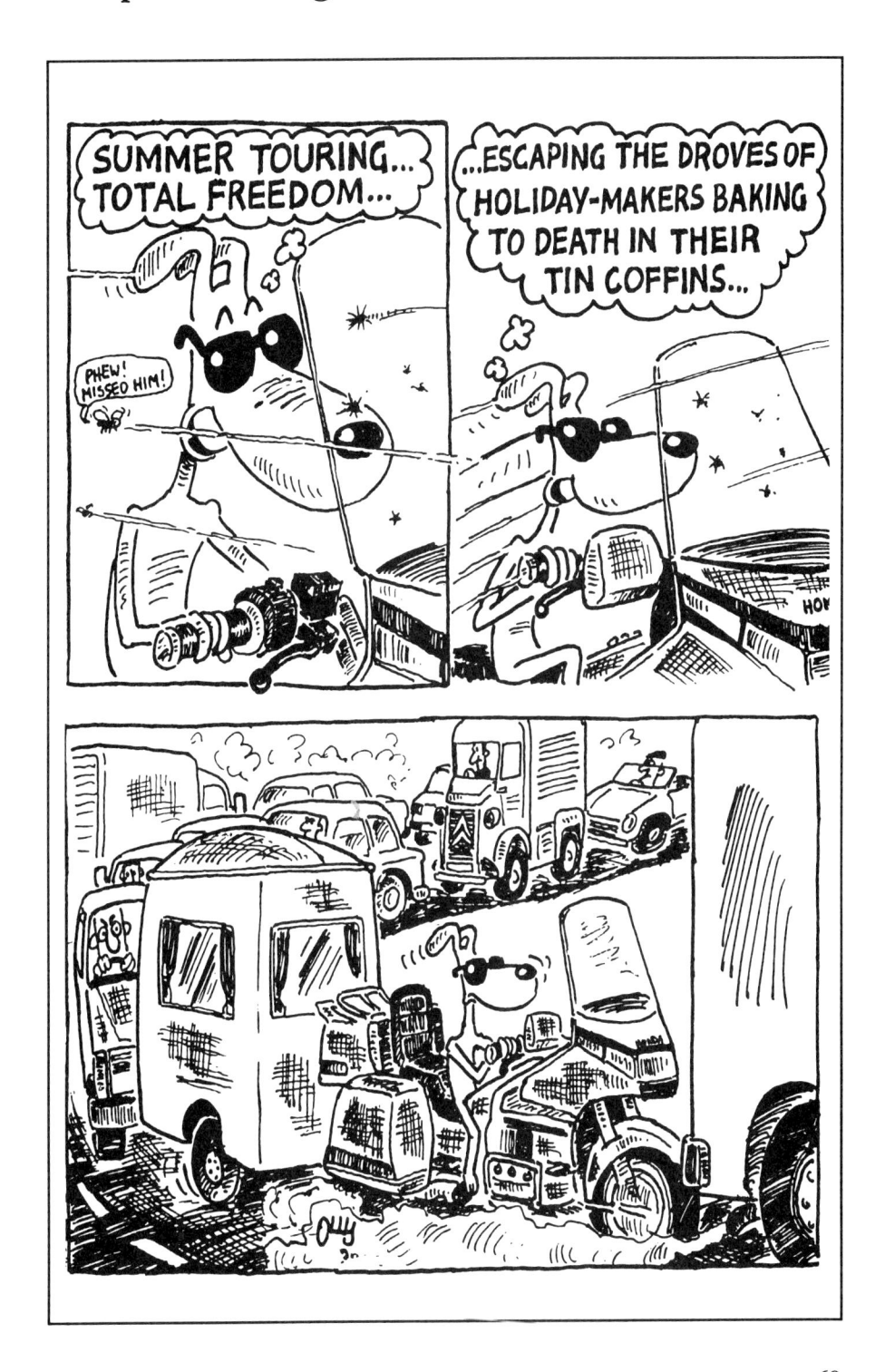

8
Touring The Great Unknown

"Although I've been biking for several years, I've never had the bottle to try touring. It's all a bit daunting and so I've taken the easy way out and have just done short trips of less than a day. I'm jealous of those bikers who manage to tour abroad."
Sally, 36 years.

To some, the idea of touring conjures up images of boring old farts, tootling along on overweight motorcycles and lecturing the bored, pillion-mounted missus over the intercom. Touring need not be like that at all. Indeed, it isn't. It's vibrant and exciting. Every tour is an adventure.

And don't be daunted by the prospect of foreign lingos, foreign foods and the big unknown. Continental cafés, great wines, empty roads and stunning scenery are all there for you to savour. What's more, when you're on a bike you make friends wherever you go, and the courtesy shown by drivers is something you rarely see in this country. Even the police can be friendly. Two mates and I were once stopped by the French gendarmes, only to go through an inquisition about the bikes we were riding. The fact that we were doing well over the ton was irrelevant!

On Your Way

There's something almost sacred about boarding the ferry to the Continent. As the boat leaves our shores and the British mainland recedes into the horizon, a small shiver goes down your spine. You've made the break. You settle down to some fish 'n' chips, have a drink and stare dreamily at the maps and your planned routes. Your holiday has begun – and you know you're about to have the experience of a lifetime. It doesn't matter how many times you make the journey, the feeling is always the same. You've left behind the worry about the lack of office paperclips and you're about to taste freedom.

Part of the thrill is embarking on the unknown. The languages, cultures, architectures, scenery and foods are all so different. You meet new people, happen upon village fetes, discover tucked-away restaurants and ride brilliant roads. Every day brings a new adventure and, because you're a biker, drunken Frenchmen spout tales of two-wheeled glory from their distant youth.

There's a fundamental difference between the British and the Continentals: the latter are brought up on two wheels. By the age of 14 most of them are riding mopeds and, even if they progress to four wheels, they never forget the thrill of biking and always appreciate the dangers. Wherever you go, whenever you stop, someone will want to chat about your machine. And with the exception of the odd turbo-charged nutter, Continental drivers are extremely courteous to motorcyclists. While you're made to feel a leather-clad hooligan in Britain, you receive a warm welcome abroad. Read on, to find out how you can have a taste of the good life.

FRENCH COPS ARE BIKER-FRIENDLY

What Bikes Are Good For Touring?

The answer is simple: take whatever you own. It doesn't matter if you have a scooter, a race replica or a bulky tourer, they all do the same job, but in different ways. The first myth to blast is the one that sportsters are uncomfortable. They're not. Your body is great at adapting and, if you're used to the bum-in-the-air riding position, you'll have no problems. Your luggage-carrying capacity will be restricted, but once you hit the twisties you won't want to be burdened anyway.

Tourers may be great at gobbling up the miles on straight roads, but they're severely disadvantaged when they're faced with Alpine passes. Unfaired bikes are generally comfortable, but without wind protection they can be hard work if you want to make good headway, and riding into a headwind for a full day will leave you shattered.

Sports-tourers, such as Honda's Blackbird and Kawasaki's ZZ-R1100, are an excellent compromise between tourer and sportster, although even humble commuters can be pleasant if you take your time. Custom bikes are tough work; their lack of wind protection, combined with the way you're seated, makes them very uncomfortable.

Can I Travel Two-Up?

There's nothing worse than sitting on the back of a high-speed bike, being buffeted by the turbulence, busting for a pee and wishing you'd stopped at that quaint little café your other half probably didn't even see.

Two-up touring is different to travelling on your own. When you're at the controls, you're concentrating on what you enjoy, riding a bike; when you're riding pillion, you really want to gaze lovingly at the scenery.

If you wish to go high-speed touring, scratch mountainous roads and experience the thrill of a lifetime, don't take your partner. It's unfair on them. It won't be what you really want either, because your machine's performance will be seriously compromised by that lump on the back. Meanwhile, the person seated behind you probably won't relish your over-exuberance and your eagerness to forge relentlessly ahead. They want to see the countryside, sample the local life and feel like a human being at the end of the day.

If you do decide to take a biking holiday together, the type of motorcycle you ride matters very much. Race replicas are a definite no-no, for starters. You'll need a machine with adequate pillion leg room and seating space, plus the ability to carry the extra luggage. Sports-tourers, big retros, tourers and big trail bikes are ideal.

You'll also probably have to stop more frequently. Although you may not realise it, as the rider you are physically quite active and your concentration is absorbed, so you might not appreciate just how uncomfortable sitting still on the back of a bike can be. The pillion suffers more from wind noise and turbulence, so you'll also have to keep your speed down.

And unless a thump in the back is your preferred method of communication, try an intercom (see Chapter 14). If you don't have an intercom, use ear plugs to cut down on the wind noise and the possibility of damaging your hearing.

What Documents Do I Need?

Basic Papers: You'll have to take your passport, driving licence, bike registration papers and insurance papers as a minimum. A Green Card is not absolutely necessary. Going abroad with the minimum is all very well if nothing untoward happens, but it could equally land you in all sorts of trouble should things not go as planned.

Bike Insurance: If you are comprehensively insured, some companies automatically provide comprehensive Euro-cover, while others will only cover you for third party, fire and theft while abroad, and you'll need a Green Card to extend your cover back to comprehensive. Check before you leave.

Medical Insurance: It makes sense to take this out when you are abroad. Although you probably wouldn't be charged for a stay in hospital while abroad, you might well have to pay for the paramedics to scrape you off the road. As well as covering any such costs, medical insurance will provide an air ambulance to fly you home in case of serious injury, or in the worst-case scenario will cart your body back. An E111 certificate (available from the post office) is advisable, as it can assist in getting medical care from a hospital.

Additional Bike Cover: This is a must. If your bike breaks down, or is made unrideable because of a crash – and you don't have a get-you-home policy – you could find yourself with a real headache. A good policy will provide roadside assistance and will make sure your pride and joy is transported home if it's beyond repair, plus provide you with a hire car and accommodation.

Money: Most credit cards are valid throughout Europe, but check with your bank first. It's worth taking a bundle of notes for coffees and meals, motorway tolls and general spending. Travellers cheques are handy. If you are relying on plastic, cost out the holiday before you go and make sure your account will stand the damage – the last thing you want is to have your card refused before the end of the holiday. As a rule of thumb, reckon on £20 per night per person for an average hotel; £20 per person per day for coffees, lunch and an evening meal; estimate your fuel costs (most bikes average around 35 to 40mpg); add the cost of the return ferry/Channel Tunnel; and include a bit for holiday expenses. On top of that you'll need to add such things as travel insurance.

How Do I Cross The Channel?

You can either use the ferry or the tunnel. The advantage of the Dover-Calais Shuttle is that it's quick (crossing time about 30 minutes), but bikers have to either stand by their machines or sit on the floor of the train (there's no seating available). Bikes are secured by a front wheel clamp, which allows the machine to rock slightly, but is stable.

Prices for Le Shuttle range from around £80 for a five-day return for rider, pillion and motorcycle (leaving early morning) to around £250 for over five days, travelling during the weekend at high season. The Dover-Calais ferry crossing takes around one hour and 20 minutes, but there are restaurants, bars and comfy seats available. P&O Stena lines charges from around £75 for a five-day return and up to about £155 for an open-ended, high-season return, making the boat the cheaper option. I'd recommend travelling by boat. Boarding is easy and tie-downs are provided to secure your bike.

Alternatively you can make the Portsmouth-Le Havre or Portsmouth-St.Malo overnight ferry, which sets sail at around 8pm and docks at around 7am the next day. Cabins are available at reasonable prices and the boats are luxurious. A five-day return crossing for rider, pillion and bike with P&O Portsmouth costs around £85 in high season, while an open-ended return crossing costs around £100. The beauty of landing in Le Havre is that you cut out the boring roads and scenery in northern France and are immediately absorbed into lovely countryside.

How Far Can I Travel?

Europe's a big place, with a huge variety of places to see. But if you take a one or two-week break, you won't be able to travel huge distances. Decide which countries you wish to visit and plan your routes accordingly. Remember that journeys usually take longer than you expect. After stopping for fuel, coffees and lunches, you'll be amazed at how slow your average speed will be – almost certainly less than 50mph.

Most people will find 300 miles a day sufficient, and even that can be tiring. You might be sitting still on the bike, but the buffeting, wind noise and concentration will drain you.

What About Accommodation?

When you begin to feel tired towards the end of the day, decide which town you wish to stop at and then look around for an appropriate hotel. Even in high summer you'd be unlucky not to find a room.

Hotels are generally cheaper abroad than at home, with prices starting at around £15 per room. Le patron will almost certainly have owned a moped or bike at some stage in his life (as will the staff), so you will be welcomed. Most hotels will find a corner of the family garage where you can leave your machine for the night, but it's advisable to take a lock in case you're forced to leave it outside.

What Kit Should I Take?

If you're travelling during the summer, take the minimum that you think you can get away with. A heavily-loaded bike is cumbersome to handle, and you'll have to cart all your luggage into the hotel each night. I recommend wearing leathers for protection, but also carry a lightweight, one-piece waterproof suit. After that it's down to how frugal you are.

TRAVEL LIGHT...

If you are travelling on your own, you should be able to pack your clothes into a small bag that can be strapped onto the pillion seat. A tank bag is extremely useful for carrying valuables, papers and odd bits you may want to get at during the day. Tank bags also have map holders, so you won't have to keep fumbling in your pockets to extract battered maps. Also, while you may risk leaving smelly T-shirts and socks unguarded in your luggage, you can carry a tank bag with you. You'll need panniers if you're holidaying two-up.

Always take some form of bike lock and fit an alarm system to the bike. A basic tool kit is useful (enough to adjust the chain and carry out minor repairs) and don't forget a can of chain lube and a puncture repair kit. You should also carry spare light bulbs and your bike should display a GB sticker.

Which Are The Best Countries For Biking?

As a rule of thumb, the northerly European countries are more heavily populated and industrialised than those further south, and they suffer from more rain and cold. Holland, for instance, is criss-crossed by a maze of motorways, the scenery is flat and the roads uninteresting. Belgium is very built up and desolate, while northern Germany is dull. By heading south you will be assured of more sunshine and warmth, superb roads and lovely scenery.

<u>France</u>: This is the obvious choice for biking, with every type of road you could wish for, and the further south you go the better it gets. And it's just a hop over the Channel. Even though the Dover-Calais crossing is the quickest and cheapest, the area just south of Calais is pretty bleak and the roads straight. The ferries from Portsmouth to Le Havre, Caen or St Malo drop you straight into quintessential France, with lush, undulating countryside and swooping roads, but don't expect the weather in the north to be much better than in Britain.

Once you reach the middle of the country – around Limoges and Clermont-Ferrand – you hit bikers' paradise. Equally, on the eastern side of the country, south of Dijon, the roads leading up to the Jura mountain range are fabulous. The west coast roads, leading down to Bordeaux, are fairly uninteresting.

Southern France is where it's at. Forget the trendy, built-up part east of Marseilles and head towards the Pyrenees. There are numerous twisty, scenic routes leading south from Limoges and Clermont to the mountains. Just look at a map, pick the twistiest bits of Tarmac and get rolling! Once in the Pyrenees you'll have the experience of a lifetime, with little traffic, well-surfaced, extremely grippy roads, and dramatic views. Just watch where you're going, though, because overshooting a bend can either send you into a cliff face or over the edge. What's more, you're on the border with Spain.

Switzerland: There's more to Switzerland than cows, cuckoo clocks and chocolate, like hundreds of Alpine passes that will blow your mind. The country may be pricey, but a look at the map will reveal superb mountain roads and scenery that is even more dramatic than the Pyrenees. However, there's one big difference between France and Switzerland: while the French are laid-back and the police relatively friendly towards bikers, the Swiss are far more austere and the cops strict as hell. Avoid the Swiss motorways too, because the autoroute passes are valid for one year only and cost a bundle.

If you're willing to gun it you can reach the Geneva or Lausanne area in a day from Calais, but you'll have a more pleasant journey if you stop off around Dijon. Then head towards Martigny-Ville, slightly southeast of the eastern end of Lake Geneva, which is near both the St Bernard and Simplon passes that take you into Italy. After negotiating the St Bernard pass and dropping down to Aosta, head west over the Col du Petit St Bernard (another pass) and back into France, where you'll discover yet more mountain passes.

Don't forget central Switzerland. East of Martigny lies a host of Alpine passes to whet your appetite. This is an area where you can ride up to five passes in a day! Now if that's not enough to tempt you, you're better off tending to your cabbage patch.

Italy: Northern Italy hosts the southern edge of the Alps and has beautiful lakes by the score. The easiest access is through Switzerland and the Simplon pass, which takes you straight into the lakes area, where you ride the edges of Lake Maggiore, Lake Lugano, Lake Como and Lake Lecco, to name but a few. The Italians are friendly, their driving somewhat erratic and their food excellent. Unfortunately northern Italy is heavily industrialised and many of the roads are very busy, so keep clear of the Milan complex.

If you're into sightseeing, this area is only a day's ride from Genoa,

Pisa, Florence and Bologna. Once you leave the main arteries, you can bury yourself in the countryside, where you find delightful villages, good restaurants and pleasant roads.

Spain: If you're in the French Pyrenees, Spain is just a stone's throw away. And like the French, Spaniards are bike-mad, but the police can be very heavy-handed. It's advisable to take out a Bail Bond when riding in Spain, as if you're involved in an accident, or are stopped for speeding, the police can impound your bike. Bail Bonds are linked to your insurance and can be bought from your insurance company, and allow you to continue riding.

Plan the correct route in the Spanish Pyrenees and you'll have a terrific time, but the roads are a mixed blessing: some are well-surfaced, others are abysmal. It's generally best to stick to the national roads (those marked in red), because otherwise you may find yourself on badly-surfaced Tarmac. There are also some great coastal rides along the Mediterranean.

The alternative entry to Spain is to take the 24-hour ferry from Portsmouth to Santander, from where you can ride into the Atlantic Pyrenees via the bull-fighting town of Pamplona, or from the coastal town of San Sebastian. However, the Atlantic Pyrenees don't offer the wonderful roads of the Eastern Pyrenees, and the countryside is much starker than that of France, but your return journey to Britain can take you through the Dordogne, with its lush, hilly countryside.

A word of warning: Although the Continental police can be lenient towards speeding bikers, a disgruntled copper can just as easily slap an instant fine on you. The French spot fine is about 900 francs (£90) and, if you don't have the cash to pay up, your bike will be taken to the nearest police station until you rustle up the money.

Ten Tips For Touring

1. Make a check-list of the things you need to take, for example passport, driving licence, etc, and tick each item off as you pack it.
2. Leave plenty of time to board the ferry/Le Shuttle.
3. Decide how far you wish to travel each day and plan your route accordingly.
4. Carry the minimum luggage. A tank bag is useful because it can both display your map and hold valuables you won't want to leave on the

bike while it's parked up.
5. Wear ear plugs. Constant wind noise can harm your hearing. Take spare ear plugs.
6. Carry a visor cleaning kit (small container of soapy water and a soft cloth will do) in your tank bag.
7. Stop riding whenever you feel weary. A loss of concentration could be fatal.
8. Use the correct side of the road. Everyone does it – they stop and then set off, riding on the left-hand side of the road. This can be very dangerous. Write a note to yourself and stick it next to the clocks.
9. If oncoming drivers flash you, that means there are police ahead. The Continentals are very good at warning bikers about speed traps, so take heed.
10. Stop plenty, stroll around, relax. You're on holiday now!

Chapter 9: Fast 'n' Furious: Track Days

9
Fast 'n' Furious: Track Days

"To see those bikers zoom round the track makes me feel very timid. I'd love to have a go, but have never managed to work up enough courage. A few of my friends spent a day at the track and they had a great time, so maybe I'll try it one day."
Peter, 41 years.

The adrenaline's pumping, your eyes are bulging with a mixture of fear and concentration, you're hurtling into a bend faster than you've ever dared to before, you slam your machine onto its side, power out of the corner...and wonder why you haven't taken part in a track day before. When you return to the paddock at the end of your session you're a gibbering wreck, laughing, recounting tales of derring-do to your mates, and feeling like a pumped-up teenager.

Apart from the excitement, there's another very good reason you should ride race circuits: it teaches you how to handle your machine at speed. You'll never learn the fine art of bike control on the road (unless you're a complete lunatic) and owning a powerful motorcycle goes hand-in-glove with – dare I say it? – fast road riding.

Mental Preparation

Most riders crap themselves before their first track day. Somehow the image of on-the-edge racers and rag-doll bodies flying through the air obliterates logic, and you can't think straight. You're frightened that you'll make a complete fool of yourself, that you'll crash, that everyone else will be a finely-honed expert. And naturally you're concerned that some hooligan will T-bone you as you enter the next bend – and destroy your bike.

Look at it another way. Track days attract everyone from experienced road racers to complete novices, so there's almost bound to be someone else who's slower than you. There's no general traffic, everyone's circulating in the same direction, there are marshals to warn you if danger lies ahead, and you'll be placed in a group that's on a par with your riding skills. Few people crash, and the ones that do so are generally the fast riders who almost certainly won't be in your group and who are travelling at racing speed. If the worst happens, there's a staffed medical centre and an ambulance standing by, ready to whisk you off to the nearest hospital, which is more than you can expect on the road.

You need to be mentally alert when you get out there, but you don't want to be so hyped up that you freeze with fear. If your body is rigid with anticipation, you won't ride well. You should be relaxed, but keen. Make the grey matter understand that what you're about to do is relatively safe (and actually safer than riding on the road) and that you're going both for the thrills and the experience.

Everyone has their own method for sorting out their brain and body before going on the track. You can try talking to yourself, breathing deeply, or forcing your body to go limp.

Machine Preparation

Before anyone goes road racing, their machine is thoroughly checked over by scrutineers. This is for everyone's safety. Some track day companies are starting to do this, but you should have given your bike an inspection before you take part. Preparing your bike gives you a better understanding about how it works and it helps with your mental preparation. If you have a friendly dealer, get the mechanic to go through the bike with you should you not feel confident about checking it on your own.

Look at the following:

<u>Brakes</u>: There should be plenty of meat on the pads. If necessary, fit new brake pads before you arrive at the circuit. If you fit new pads at the circuit, give them time to scrub in before you start going fast. Make sure both front and rear brakes are working properly.

<u>Chain</u>: Tension your chain correctly. Lube it, but be careful not to spray on too much oil, because excessive lubrication will result in chain oil being flung onto the rear tyre, which is not a good idea. It's best to lubricate your chain the night before, to let the oil soak in. If there's oil on the rear tyre when you arrive at the track, wipe it off with a cloth lightly damped in petrol.

Engine: Check the oil level. If you're riding a two-stroke, for heaven's sake make sure the oil tank isn't about to run dry. Two-strokes have a horrible habit of seizing just as you're reaching maximum speed.

Tyres: Make sure there's plenty of tread and that the treads aren't stepped. Good-condition rubber grips better and makes your bike handle better. Check your tyre pressures. If you reckon you're going to be handy on the circuit, fit race-compound rubber, as it has far more grip than normal road rubber. Racing tyres normally run at lower pressures than road tyres, so ask the manufacturer for the recommended pressures for track work.

General: Give your bike a good clean before the track day and while you're doing so make sure there are no loose nuts and bolts. Be sure in your mind that your bike is in tip-top condition.

GET TO KNOW YOUR BIKE ON TRACK DAYS...

Preparing Yourself

As a first-timer you're going to be nervous before your date with the track. You might feel you're about to flirt with death, but nothing could be further from the truth; in fact you're in far greater danger riding to and from the circuit. Ironically, many racers don't like road riding, precisely because they feel it's too risky!

On the road you're at the mercy of other drivers and, even if you don't come into contact with a vehicle if you have an accident, there's a host of other potentially fatal objects to hit, like kerbing, signs, walls, trees, bollards and the like. Race tracks have run-off areas around the danger zones, so if you do fall off you normally simply slide to a halt without hitting anything. And of course medical help is always instant.

Still slightly nervous? Well, that's not a bad thing, because you certainly don't want to be over-confident, although your body should be relaxed and your mind alert.

Don't forget the deep breathing exercises before you go out on the circuit and, if you feel your body stiffening up while riding the track, start the deep breathing again. Above all, get out there with a sense of fun – after all, that's probably why you decided to take part in the first place!

Most track day companies are advertised in the bike press and popular circuits become fully booked well in advance. The company will give you all the details, such as what time to arrive at the circuit, how many people will be taking part, and how long you can reasonably expect to have on the track. Prices for track days range from around £65 to £140, depending on the time of year and the circuit.

... BY PUSHING IT...

What To Expect

Apart from the fun and thrills, a day at the circuit is a very sociable experience, because you're mingling with like-minded folk. Most people will have ridden their bikes to the circuit and obviously want to ride them home again. The cutting-edge stuff starts when you're hooked – now you'll want a machine specially for the track and arrive in a van.

The day starts with signing-on, your decision about which group to join in (normally fast, medium or slow) and a briefing, where you'll be told about how to ride the circuit, what the flags mean if they are waved by the marshals and what to do in case of an accident. As a first-timer in the slow group, you will be led round the track by an instructor for (usually) your first two sessions to give you an idea of the circuit's layout.

After that you'll be free to ride on your own, although the instructors are normally available to help you out whenever you wish.

Building Up Speed

It's all too easy to push hard on cold tyres and slide off early in a session. Let your tyres warm up for a couple of laps at the start of each session before you push the bike, which will give you time to orientate yourself with the track. You have the whole day ahead, so increase your speed gradually through each session and ride within your limits. Your knowledge of the circuit will improve with every outing.

...TO THE ABSOLUTE LIMIT

When you begin to feel more confident later in the day, try to remember the gears for each section, your braking point markers and turn-in, apex and exit points for the corners. The problem is that as you build up speed, your perception of the track will change, which can catch you out. As a first-timer you'll probably suffer from the following:

Common Problem: You become fixated with the track immediately in front of you instead of looking ahead. This is usually due to nerves. It's not unusual for people to run off at corners, only because they've been staring at the Tarmac just ahead of their front wheel.
What To Do: Relax and look well ahead.

Common Problem: You become fixated with the bike in front of you and follow it slavishly. This again is down to nerves. Remember, the riders ahead may have no idea where they are going.

What To Do: Just as you would on the road, be aware of what's happening immediately in front of you, but still keep looking well ahead. If a bike crashes in front of you, it usually spins clear.

Common Problem: You road ride, looking over you shoulder or into your mirrors before entering a bend.
What To Do: Don't even think about what's behind you, keep your concentration pinned on the track ahead. On the circuit the rider in front has the right of way.

Common Problem: You get 'sucked' into corners, which means you turn into bends too early and run out of road on the exit. You then might have the unpleasant choice of having to scrub off speed by braking, or turning in tighter on the exit, or running off the track.
What To Do: Try turning each corner into a perfect arc, with just one steering change of direction at the entry.

Common Problem: You're jerky with the throttle, rolling it on and off through bends. This upsets the suspension and makes the bike unstable.
What To Do: Try to be as smooth as possible with the throttle and, once you've released the brakes on entering a corner, roll on the throttle gradually.

Common Problem: You sit on the bike like a sack of spuds, arms stretching to the handlebars like rigid rods.
What To Do: You should be supple, with arms bent and relaxed, head down, feet placed tip-toed on the footpegs and upper body ready to lean into the direction you're steering the bike. You don't see professional riders sitting bolt upright during a race – and that's because they use their body weight to help control the bike.

Once you've started to learn the track, make notes about what you do and where you do it. Talk yourself through a typical lap, working out where you are making mistakes and what you need to do to improve your skills. As you progress, you can begin to work out the best lines, later braking points and where you should get on the power. You won't increase your lap times and ability unless you think logically.

Pester the instructors for information and get them to take you round. Your mind should be like a sponge, desperate for information.

Track days are not just physically tiring – they're mentally exhausting too.

Chapter 12 is devoted to advanced riding techniques. Have a read of it before your track day.

Which Tracks Are Best?

The most common circuits booked for track days are Cadwell Park, Mallory Park, Oulton Park and Snetterton. Brands Hatch and Donington Park are hugely popular, but are more expensive to rent and are therefore used less. If you're wondering which circuits you should try out, here's a brief description of the main ones you're most likely to ride:

Brands Hatch (near Fawkham, Kent. Tel: 01474 872331)
Everyone wants to ride Brands, especially the GP circuit. It has been the scene of some epic World Superbike battles and a firm favourite with spectators. The full circuit is just over 2.6 miles long, with the scariest, blind, high-speed bend you could dream of – Paddock Hill. The rest of the track is tricky too, because it undulates and takes in both fast and slow-ish corners that are extremely demanding.

The GP circuit is fast, so you need to know what you're doing before you start pushing yourself too hard. A must, but track days here tend to be more expensive than elsewhere. The Indy, or short circuit is fun too, even though it's just over 1.2 miles long. You still have the thrill of Paddock Hill bend, plus some good high-side potential when you return to the start-finish straight off Clearways.

Cadwell Park (near Louth, Lincs. Tel: 01507 343248)
The full circuit is 2.17 miles long and incorporates the famous Mountain, where top racers become airborne and overzealous novices flip their bikes. The circuit is hilly, with both tight and sweeping corners. The start-finish straight leads out into the countryside, where there's plenty of run-off, but the Woodland section is narrow and the run-off limited. However, it's the Woodland section that's really exciting; get it right and it's exhilarating, get it wrong and they'll be untangling you from the Armco.

The short circuit is just under 1.5 miles and leaves out the Woodland section. It has some technical corners, like the downhill right-left flick of the Gooseneck and the double-apex right-hander of Charlie's, but it's not a patch on the full circuit.

Donington Park (near Derby, Derbyshire. Tel: 01332 810048)

This has been the home of the British motorcycle grand prix for years, Donington Park is a natural crowd-puller. In terms of facilities it's on a par with the best European circuits, but it's not as fast as many of them. It is quick by British standards, however, with plenty of run-off and corners that flow naturally from one to the other.

The drive down through Craner Curves, at around 120mph, is sensational, and the drive onto the back straight (under the Dunlop Bridge) a real test of throttle control. This is a great track to ride, but it lacks the intimacy and atmosphere of Cadwell or Oulton. The GP, or full circuit is 2.5 miles, while the 1.95-mile National circuit simply lops off the Melbourne Loop, which is no great loss.

Knockhill (near Dunfermline, Fife. Tel: 01383 723337)

Scotland's circuit is short, tight and challenging. It's also hilly and narrow, with blind bends and crests, and a fairly short start-finish straight, which means there's no time to relax. It's the circuit equivalent to a B-road (but with good run-off) so it's a scratcher's paradise, although you might wonder how a full grid of Superbikes copes on the 1.3 miles of twisty Tarmac!

Mallory Park (near Hinckley, Leics. Tel: 01455 842931)

At just 1.3 miles long, Mallory is a short track that's dominated by the seemingly never-ending, 100-mph corner of Gerard's. It's a nominally easy circuit to learn, although your entry speed into Gerard's is largely down to your bottle. The fast right-left flick through the Lake Esses is where the quick lads slide off, and off-camber Devil's Elbow, leading onto the main straight is prime highside territory.

Oulton Park (near Chester, Cheshire. Tel: 01829 760301)

This is one superb circuit. At 2.77 miles it's also one of the longer tracks you're likely to ride, and it's extremely technical. For many bikers the Oulton experience beats both Brands and Donington. The track undulates through the countryside, past a scenic country lake and into the woodland section that can remain damp when the rest of the Tarmac has dried out. There's a banked hairpin, a chicane, sweeping corners and tight bends.

Ripples in the track have the front wheel becoming airborne under acceleration, while the front end goes all light over Deer's Leap, the crested left-hander leading onto the start-finish straight. Lack of run-off in the woodland section calls for some caution, but the rest of the track has plenty. Get one corner wrong and you'll definitely mess up the next few. A must.

Pembrey (near Llanelli, Carmarthenshire. Tel: 01554 891042)
This is a smashing little track. It may be flat and only 1.45 miles long, but it twists and turns, never giving you a rest. You enter the short start-finish straight hard on the throttle, which is followed by fierce braking into a hairpin. The ensuing series of left and right-hand bends keeps you on your toes.

Snetterton (near Thetford, Norfolk. Tel: 01953 887303)
This is where big-bike owners can make real use of their high-powered machines, reaching up to 160mph on the back straight before braking hard into the left-right Esses. It may be thrilling watching the speedo, but don't take your eyes off the track for long, because the corners come rushing up real fast! The 1.95-mile circuit also incorporates slow and high-speed bends, and a silly chicane that completely breaks your rhythm. A must for speed freaks.

Thruxton (near Andover, Hants. Tel: 01264 772696)
Fast, wide and flat, virtually all of Thruxton's bends call for courage and more than a little nerve once you start going for it. Take Church Corner, for example, which is well over 100mph, knee-down, with the bike dancing around over the bumps. The 2.35-mile track does have its heavy braking points and tight bends, but it's the quick sections you remember. Unlike Oulton or Cadwell, the venue is bleak, but you won't leave disappointed.

Track–Day Action Plan

1. Decide which track(s) you want to ride and book ahead. Don't expect to turn up on the day and ride.
2. Prepare your bike. For everyone's safety, it should be in tip-top condition.
3. You'll need either a one-piece set of leathers, or a two-piece set that zips together. Your leathers, boots and gloves shouldn't be holed. If your helmet has been crashed, buy a new one.

4. Arrive at the circuit in time for the briefing, especially if it's your first outing.
5. Stay the previous night at a local B&B if you live a long way from the circuit. You don't want a tiring ride before you arrive – and don't forget, you have to ride home too.
6. When you've started learning the track, talk yourself through a typical lap and work out your weak points. Then work on them.
7. Make full use of the instructors.
8. Don't rush out and crash during your first few laps. Build up your speed during the day.
9. Let your tyres warm up for the first couple of laps of each session.
10. Relax and enjoy the day.

Chapter 10: Basic Maintenance

10
Basic Maintenance

"I never look under the bonnet of my car, and I treat my bike the same. I love riding it, but I haven't a clue about mechanics. I don't even know how to adjust the chain."
Ian, 31 years.

Your car is a boring, soulless, yet comfortable method of transporting you and your family from A to B. There's no reason to understand why, or how, it works. It just does. You take it to the garage to have it serviced and you call the AA or RAC when it breaks down.

One reason you became a born-again biker and bought a motorcycle was because you wanted to break out of your tin can and push the boundaries of excitement. But bikes are not like cars. You can drive around with a half-flat tyre on a car and not notice it, but low tyre pressure on a motorcycle critically affects the handling. And if you don't oil the bike's chain, for example, it will rust, links will seize and it would then be likely to snap, which could cause enormous damage to you and your machine.

In any case, understanding how your bike works is fundamental to good riding. You needn't become an expert mechanic, but there are times when you're going to have to get those hands dirty.

Using The Centre Stand

Although you don't need brawn to hoist your bike onto its centre stand, you do need a bit of brain; there is a knack to it. If you've collapsed in a heap along side your bike in a futile attempt, don't feel ashamed – you're not the only one. Here's how to get your bike on the centre stand:
1. Stop the engine and put the bike into neutral. Grab the front brake firmly.

2. Push the side stand down with your left foot and tilt the bike onto the stand.
3. Get off the bike, still holding the brake lever, making sure the side stand is fully extended.
4. Grab the left handlebar and pillion grab handle (or subframe), and push the centre stand down with your foot until it touches the ground.
5. With your foot still on the centre stand's curved tail, tilt the bike upright.
6. Place all your weight onto the centre stand and pull the bike up while gripping it firmly.
7. When the bike is as high as it's going to go, pull it backwards. You've done it!

And here's how to get the bike off its centre stand:
1. Push the side stand down, until you are sure it is fully extended and is resting solidly on the ground.
2. Holding the left handlebar and rear of the bike, pull the machine forward, with the front wheel pointing to the left.
3. Ease the bike down off the centre stand and then gently rest it on the side stand.

Using A Paddock Stand

Most bikes these days do not have centre stands, which makes simple tasks like lubricating the chain or cleaning the machine far harder. It's well worth buying a paddock stand, but it can be difficult to prop the bike on to it if you're on your own. Here's how to get your bike on a paddock stand:
1. With the bike resting on the side stand, run the paddock stand under the swingarm.
2. Adjust the lugs of the stand, so they are correctly-spaced to fit on each arm of the swingarm (if you own a bike with a single-sided swingarm, you'll have to buy a specially-adapted stand, with a lug that slips straight into the wheel hub).
3. Holding the pillion grab rail or rear of the bike with your left hand, push down on the paddock stand with your right foot, so the left lug starts to take the weight of the bike.
4. If you and the bike are stable at this stage, push down hard on the

stand. The bike will right itself, with both arms of the swingarm resting on the lugs. Continue pushing so the stand slides into place.

And here's how to get the bike off the paddock stand:
1. Make sure the side stand is down.
2. Gently pull up on the paddock stand's tail and lower the rear wheel to the ground, keeping the bike balanced with the stand.
3. Steadying the bike with your left hand, continue lowering the stand while tilting the bike to the left.
4. Allow the bike to drop gently onto its side stand.

Bump-Starting Your Bike

If some sports bikes are left idle for a few days with the alarm activated, the battery will run down and they have to be bump-started. If your bike won't start, do the following:
- Check that there's enough fuel in the tank and turn the fuel switch to reserve, just to be sure.
- Turn off the light switch or heated grips, or anything else that drains power.
- Find a friend.
- Turn the ignition on and add some choke.
- Sit on the bike, click into second gear and pull the clutch in.
- Shout at your mate to start pushing and start paddling yourself.
- Stand on the footpegs once near full momentum.
- As your perspiring companion breaks out in full sweat and reaches top speed, dump the clutch and drop back into the saddle at the same time. If the wheel locks up, try again in third gear.

Cleaning And Lubing The Chain

If you allow the chain to become rusty, it will wear out in no time and you'll have the expensive job of replacing it. A knackered chain is also more prone to snapping, which could be dangerous. Clean the chain from time to time and always keep it lubricated with chain lube.

If your bike doesn't have a centre stand it's a good idea to buy a paddock stand. A paddock stand lifts the rear wheel off the ground, making cleaning and maintenance much easier. As a last resort, get a friend to help you: rest the bike on its side stand and ask your friend to tip the machine towards its left side so the side stand lifts the rear wheel.

To clean the chain, soak it with engine cleaner. If you use paraffin, make sure none of it drips onto the tyre, as it will damage the compound and make it very slippery. Then scrub the chain with a brush and wash it down thoroughly with a hose. The next stage is to lube it. As soon as the chain is dry (wipe with a cloth if necessary) lube it with chain lube (which you buy in a bike shop). Spin the rear wheel with your right hand while spraying the lube with your left. Try to spray the lube lightly onto the chain's lower run, making sure none of it touches the rear tyre, and wipe off any excess lube from the chain with an old rag.

ALWAYS KEEP YOUR BIKE CLEAN

Adjusting The Chain

Keeping the drive chain correctly tensioned is important. Too much slack and it can jump around on the sprockets and possibly damage parts of the bike; too tight and it can wreck the sprockets and bearings. Preferably place the bike on its centre stand, or a paddock stand, before starting work.

Here's how to tension the chain. While feeling for play in the chain, turn the rear wheel until the chain is at its tightest. This is known as the 'tight spot'. Then loosen the wheel spindle nut or otherwise (see below). Tension the chain so there's around 1.5ins of play at the tight spot. If you can find help, get a friend to sit on the bike. With the suspension compressed, there should be at least 1in of play at the tight spot. Finally, tighten all nuts and bolts.

There are three types of chain adjuster:

<u>Eccentric.</u> This type of adjuster holds the wheel spindle in an eccentric circle in the swingarm. The problem with this method is that, by moving the wheel spindle through a circle to tension the chain, it also lowers or raises the rear of the bike and thus changes the steering geometry, which affects the way the bike steers. To adjust this type, loosen the pinch bolts on both sides of the swingarm; then, using a purpose-made key, twist the eccentric adjuster round until you have the correct chain tension. Make sure the eccentric adjusters on both sides of the swingarm are identically positioned. Lastly, tighten the pinch bolts.

<u>Slot adjuster</u>. This is the conventional method of adjusting chains. It's a bit more fiddly than the eccentric adjuster, but it won't alter your steering geometry. To adjust, loosen the wheel spindle nut. At the back of the swingarm are two nuts. Loosen the outer lock nuts on both sides of the swingarm and then, using the correct spanner, wind both adjusting nuts in clockwise equal amounts (for example, half a turn each) until the chain is at the correct tension. Then look at the chain tensioner marks on either side of the swingarm and make sure they are evenly positioned. This way you'll know your wheel is straight. Tighten the wheel spindle nut hard, and nip up the lock nuts.

<u>Single-sided swingarm.</u> Bikes with single-sided swingarms have their own method of chain adjustment, and need a special C-spanner. To adjust, loosen the pinch bolts near the wheel hub; then using the C-spanner, adjust the chain by moving the whole wheel hub eccentrically. When the chain is correctly tensioned, nip up the pinch bolts.

NOTE: Certain manufacturers (Ducati for one) state that the chain must be tensioned with someone sitting on the machine. Check in your manual or with your dealer.

Lubing The Controls

Most basically, oil the brake and clutch levers, and give the brake and gearchange pedal pivot points a squirt from an oil spray can from time to time. Wipe off excess oil with a rag.

For lubing the throttle cable, undo the screws clamping the throttle-side switchgear to the handlebar. Using an oil spray can with a fine nozzle, spray oil into the cable, working the throttle to help the oil work its way down the cable. Lightly oil or grease the throttle mechanism and screw the assembly back together.

And to lube the clutch cable, remove the clutch lever locknut with a socket and unscrew the lever's pivot pin. Wind the adjuster right in, line up the slots and wiggle the cable free. Next, pull the cable from the lever and attach a cable oiler (which you can buy from an accessory shop) around the top of the cable. Stick the straw from the can of lube into the oiler and spray until the oil seeps out of the lower end of the cable. Lastly, attach the cable to the lever, refit the lever and adjust the cable.

Changing The Oil In Ten Steps

If you want to save yourself money between major services, and you're confident you can check over essentials like brake pads and chain condition, doing an oil change is dead easy. If your bike has a canister oil filter, you'll need a filter wrench, or if the filter is in a housing make sure you have the correct-sized socket or spanner. To complete the job you'll need the correct socket for the drain plug and preferably a torque wrench. Follow these ten steps:

1. Run the engine so the oil warms up.
2. Place a washing-up bowl under the sump and loosen the sump plug with the correct-sized socket.
3. Remove the sump plug and washer carefully by hand. As you pull the plug free, oil will drain out over your hand. (You may want to wear a glove.) Allow the oil to drain completely.
4. Clean the sump plug with some loo paper, then screw it back in carefully by hand and tighten with a torque wrench to the recommended torque. Otherwise nip up the plug, being careful not to over-tighten it and strip the thread.
5. Now place the bowl under the oil filter.
6. Unscrew the filter, let the oil drain and wipe the engine casing clean.

7. Put the new filter in the housing, or if it's a canister screw it in place, making sure the seals are properly positioned. Tighten as recommended.
8. Pour fresh oil in through the oil filler hole (normally on the right-hand engine casing) until it reaches the top of the oil spy glass or the top of the dipstick.
9. Start the engine and let it tick over for a minute, which fills up the oil filter. Then top up the oil level and replace the oil filler cap/dipstick.
10. Run the engine up again to check for leaks.

Taking Care Of The Fluids

The master cylinder for the front brake (which is positioned next to the throttle) has a spy glass. Check that the brake fluid is above the minimum mark. If it is, OK. If it isn't, you need to top it up.

Tie some rags round the master cylinder, as brake fluid damages paintwork. Using the correct-fitting screwdriver, unscrew the two screws that retain the master cylinder lid. Then remove the lid and the rubber seal inside and top up the reservoir with the brake fluid. Replace the rubber seal, reservoir lid and screw back into place. If your bike has a hydraulic clutch, the master cylinder reservoir is positioned next to the clutch lever. Follow the same procedure.

Inspecting And Changing Your Brake Pads

Brake pads should last between services, but if you're doing your own minor services you'll need to inspect or change them yourself. Scabby or soiled brake pads cause the discs to wear unevenly. You should clean and grease the brake calipers every 3000 miles, especially during winter when there is more dirt and salt on the roads.

Before you set to work on the calipers, check the brakes aren't binding. With the bike in neutral, squeeze the brake lever and release; if you then cannot push the bike forward easily, the front brakes are binding. Do the same with the rear brake too. Unless you are mechanically-minded, take your bike to a dealer to have the brakes serviced.

If the brakes aren't binding get to work, with the aid of a manual, on one caliper at a time. Remember that brakes are a serious business, so unless you have the necessary knowledge use a manual. Never allow the brake pads to come into contact with oil or grease and always double-check that all shims, clips, pins and bolts are properly replaced and correctly tightened. Finally, test-ride the bike before going for a blast.

Follow this ten-step guide:
1. Loosen the caliper pins that retain the pads, but do not remove. If they are seized, heat them with a blow-torch rather than forcing them.
2. Using a socket or spanner, remove the caliper-mounting bolts and wiggle the caliper free of the fork.
3. Remove the pins and any clips or shims, making a note of how they are fitted.
4. Using brake cleaner, clean out the calipers. Pump the pistons out a bit at a time (by squeezing the brake lever gently) and clean the newly-exposed sections. If the pistons are rusty, or if the pistons don't retract a little each time they are pumped out and need new seals, you should reassemble the calipers and take the bike to your dealer.
5. If the pistons are in good condition, coat them with a little brake grease.
6. Inspect the brake pads for wear, cracking or breaking up. If the pads are in bad condition, or below their wear limit, change them. If the pads are in good condition, rub them with sandpaper to remove uneven bits or glazing. Then clean the pads with brake cleaner.
7. Push the pistons back fully into the caliper, either with a G-clamp or by slipping the knackered pads back in and levering them apart.
8. Slot the new brake pads into place and replace any shims or clips. Copper-grease the pins lightly and put them back in.
9. Slide the caliper over the brake disc and wiggle back into position, then bolt it back to the fork again.
10. Pump the brake until the lever is firm, check the brake fluid level, and then set to work on the next caliper.

Make Your Bike Fit You

When you buy a new bike, it's set up for Mr Average. This may not suit you. There are various parts you can adjust, so get your spanners out...
<u>Handlebars</u>: Loosen the handlebar clamp bolts and move the bars until they feel comfortable. Tighten the clamp bolts and move the bars from lock to lock to check that they don't touch the fuel tank and don't trap your thumbs against the tank.

ALWAYS USE THE RIGHT TOOLS FOR THE JOB

Levers: Loosen the brake and clutch lever clamp bolts, and reposition the levers so your fingers feel natural while lying on them.

Lever adjusters: Some levers have span adjusters, others have a small bolt in the lever that can be adjusted. Move the adjuster until you have the desired amount of play before the lever starts to operate.

Mirrors: If necessary, loosen the mirror bolts and adjust the mirrors while you're sitting on the bike, in your normal riding position. Then tighten up the bolts.

Gear pedal: Loosen the locknuts with spanners and then turn the gear-change linkage rod to raise or lower the pedal. Sit on the bike to make sure the pedal is in the correct position.

Headlight: Unfaired bikes adjust on the main bolts, faired bikes have screw adjusters behind the reflector.

Top Tips For Good Bike Maintenance

- Clean your bike regularly, especially if you ride during the winter. It's part of getting to know the machine. Also, road salt can destroy the cosmetics in just a few months and rot exhaust pipes rapidly.
- Chrome polish and wax the bike, which helps protect the chrome and paintwork.
- If you ride during the winter, smear a thin film of grease over chromed parts, fasteners and other bits that may corrode.
- Keep the chain lubed. During wet weather you may need to lube the chain every day, as water washes the lube off.
- Check the chain tension regularly.
- Give your bike a check-over at least once a week if you ride regularly, or if you haven't taken it out for a while.
- Always use the correct tools for the job. Wrong-sized spanners, sockets and screwdrivers destroy metal edges.
- If you are inexperienced, write notes as you dismantle parts such as the brake calipers. That way you'll know in what order and position to reassemble the parts.

NOTE: Home maintenance may invalidate your warranty. Check with your dealer before working on your bike.

Chapter 11: Basic Riding Techniques

11
Basic Riding Techniques

"I've just got back on a bike after 15 years and I feel really rusty. I'm dead nervous too. My riding doesn't seem to be coming together, so I keep making mistakes. The truth is I need to start again from the beginning."
Charles, 38 years.

Resuming biking after a long break can be daunting. Not only will your basic riding skills be littered with bad habits from your youth, but there's also far more traffic on the roads these days. What's more, although modern bikes are very sophisticated, they are also far quicker, so they can easily get you into trouble. The most common bike accident used to be one where a motorcycle was hit by a car at an urban intersection; now bike accidents are more often than not solo ones, which are usually caused by excessive speed. It doesn't matter whether you've just passed your test, or whether you're a born-again, you should think seriously about taking advanced riding tuition.

Safe riding is not just about being able to control the machine. It's also about looking and thinking ahead, knowing how to relax your body, understanding speed and learning where to position your bike on the road.

MENTAL APPROACH

Stay In Credit

Riding a motorcycle is like having money in the bank. If you ride to your limit, you use up all your credit and have nothing in reserve when something goes wrong. But if you stay within your ability, your credit rating remains good and you're more likely to avoid accidents. The more credit you have, the safer you'll be.

Put it another way. When you take a corner, for example, do you commit yourself fully to getting round the bend, or are you able to make a snap decision when you spot some diesel, and avoid crashing? Anyone who rides a motorcycle to the limit of their ability is asking for trouble. Situations that pose a minor hazard to a car driver can prove fatal to a biker, so your credit is crucial.

A biker's reserve depends on their experience and skill. A good rider may be able to negotiate a bend safely at 70mph, while a novice may find the same corner daunting at 40mph. Grand prix stars can turn a motorcycle in 0.2 of a second, while the average road rider takes two seconds to do the job. Even riding down a straight road involves hundreds of decisions. If your attention is fully focused on operating the bike (like throttle control, steering or braking), you'll have no credit to react to potential hazards.

And if all this seems too obvious, the police now reckon that the majority of serious accidents are the fault of born-again bikers riding beyond their limit. Stay in credit!

Chill Out And Enjoy!

Relax, take it easy, chill out. The worst way to ride a motorcycle is to tense up, but it's still an all too common fault. A bike responds to a rider's actions; a stiff body will cause the machine to react slowly and clumsily. And when you're faced with a possible crash, it's even more important to be supple. Experienced bikers are a joy to watch, because they let their bikes flow. They are smooth because they think and act fluidly. It's because racers are physically relaxed that they are able to take their machines to the limit.

When you're tense, you grab hold of the handlebars, stab at the brakes, sit rigidly, operate the throttle jerkily and use up all your mental reserves. This means you won't steer quickly, you could end up locking the wheels, the machine won't move easily from side to side and you'll panic if anything nasty happens.

Consciously ask yourself if you're tense. Make sure your legs, your upper body - and particularly your arms - are floppy. When you're able to stay relaxed, you'll find you can control the bike better, and ride faster and more safely. For example, if the handlebars shake as your machine crests a hill or hits a bump, the worst thing you can do is to grab them, as this will cause the whole bike to wobble; hold the 'bars lightly and the motorcycle will correct itself. Or if you overcook a corner and you're sitting rigidly, the bike will run wide; relax and you'll be able to lean it further into the turn. So loosen up.

CHILL OUT WHILE RIDING

Think About It

I heard a terrible (but true) story. A biker had an accident. He bought a new motorcycle and promptly had another crash. So he bought his third machine – and soon afterwards was killed in his third successive accident. Tragically, many bikers do not learn from their mistakes. Riders who have had an accident in the previous three years are three times more likely than average to have another accident in the following year. People tend to repeat the same type of accident unless they are willing to learn from their mistakes.

According to the police, most riders involved in an accident do not accept they contributed to it. If you believe yourself to be totally blameless in a crash – and have nothing to learn from it – then you'll never improve your ability or technique. You'll continue riding as before, and most probably have another accident. The first step to becoming a better biker is to admit that you make errors. We all do, whatever our experience.

It's also very easy to become complacent and get into bad habits. Bad habits become the norm, so even though you have not had an accident you expose yourself to unnecessary danger. The second step to becoming a more proficient rider is to analyse everything you do, as you're riding along. Ask yourself if you're in the correct position on the road, if you're too close to the car in front, if you're travelling at the correct speed, what the road surface is like, or what would happen if that car pulls out from the side street.

PHYSICAL APPROACH

Stay In Contact

Don't sit like a lump - especially if you're riding a sports bike. Move your body weight around correctly and you'll find your motorcycle will respond faster and more effortlessly to your desires. But first you have to understand the contact points your body has with its machine, and why they are important.

The handlebars should be held loosely. Never grip them hard or use them to pull yourself around the bike, as this input will affect the steering. Hold them gently, keeping your elbows bent. The footpegs are not just for resting your feet on. If you want to move your body weight around, transfer your weight onto your feet. Or if your motorcycle is bouncing around over bumps, stand on the footpegs (you'll be surprised at how easily you can move on your bike by doing this). Putting all your weight onto the footpegs has another advantage: it lowers the centre of gravity of the machine, so making it more stable.

The petrol tank is an important contact point, too. Gripping the tank with your knees under hard braking, rather than pushing on the handlebars, throws less weight forward and so makes the bike more stable. For racers and sports bike riders, the tank is an important support which is gripped by the knees when cornering hard.

And finally the seat is not just for comfort. A good rider will move forward under acceleration, back under braking, and shift over to either side of the saddle when cornering (by leaning into a bend, the rider will move the mass of weight to the inside of the bike, so the machine can be kept more upright).

LOOKING AHEAD

A Vision To Survive

When you ride a motorcycle, your life depends on your eyes. What you see and how you look ahead are crucial to good biking. Many riders, especially beginners, develop tunnel vision and only stare at the road immediately in front of them. If you want to survive and ride well, you'll have to learn to be all-seeing.

The tunnel-vision biker won't notice potentially dangerous situations occurring ahead, and will almost certainly miss vehicles coming out of side streets. The most common bike accident in town is caused by cars pulling out into the path of a motorcycle. Many people's instinct is to focus on a single thing that appears to be a danger.

The most efficient method of looking ahead is by using 'wide' vision. This means you keep your eyes fixed forward, while letting your mind decide what it wants to look at. By not moving your eyes, your brain can move from object to object very quickly. You can scan the road ahead and see from side to side without your concentration being absorbed by just one thing. This is especially important in town.

It's vital to look far ahead as well; I don't mean a couple of car lengths, but right up the street if necessary. Whether you're in town or country, you should continually scan up and down the road for potential dangers. Of course the faster you ride the further ahead you should look.

Plan Your Escape

A car has pulled out on you and you're about to have an accident. Where do you look? The automatic reaction is to fix on the offending hazard, which will almost certainly mean you'll ride straight into it. This is known as target fixation. Target fixation is an instinctive reaction which blocks out escape routes. Perhaps it's only natural to be transfixed by the danger, but it's the worst thing to do. Because you've suddenly developed tunnel vision, you'll irrevocably steer towards the object you're staring at.

The only way to avoid a potential crash is to look away from it. I don't mean ignore it, but you should be aware of your options. In the split-second you have for decision-making, you'll need to identify your escape route – and go for it.

Of course you should be anticipating the worst all the time. Defensive riding makes life a whole lot easier; it ensures that you're prepared for the unexpected and have already worked out what avoiding manoeuvres you might have to take. To do this you'll need to look well ahead and have a constant overall view of your surroundings.

Bikers most likely to suffer from target fixation are those who focus on the traffic immediately ahead. They are unaware of what's taking place further up the road, they're not anticipating, they're an accident waiting to happen. If you think you're a possible victim of target fixation, start exercising your mind on how you'd avoid possible accidents while you're riding. So when the real thing happens, you'll have your escape routes sorted.

Know Where To Look

Even if you are riding down a fairly quiet urban street, there's a host of things to distract you. Side roads, pedestrians, parked cars, manhole covers and your mirrors are just some of the things that could grab your attention. So just where should your attention be focused?

Naturally you'll be scanning your surroundings, but it makes sense to concentrate on the area from which you're most at risk. Research has shown that the majority of problems we face are directly in front of us. In fact 77 per cent of accidents involving a car and a bike occur within 11 o'clock and one o'clock of the rider's forward vision.

That's because most accidents in built-up areas are caused by cars pulling across your path. For example, the car that's about to pull out of a side road or onto a roundabout (two of the most common accidents) is at 11 o'clock of your forward vision. But don't forget your flanks are still vulnerable. The slower you travel the more you need to look to your sides. At very low speeds you need to consciously pay attention to these areas, as cars, pedestrians and even dogs can then prove a greater hazard from the side.

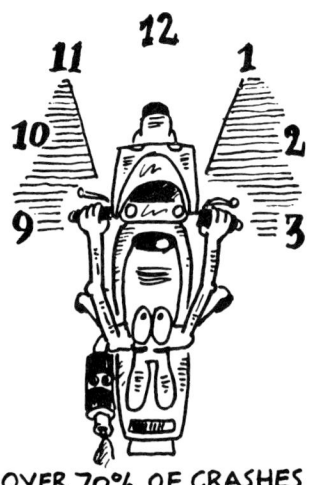

OVER 70% OF CRASHES OCCUR IN YOUR 11 O'CLOCK TO 1 O'CLOCK LINE-OF-SIGHT

That might mean turning your head, rather than using just peripheral vision. To illustrate this, take a piece of paper with writing on it and place it directly in front of you. It's easy to read. But as you move it to the side, the writing becomes increasingly blurred, even though you're still aware of its presence. There's another interesting point: as speed increases, your field of vision becomes narrower and your peripheral vision more blurred, so you'll then need to spot potential dangers well before you reach them.

Be A Biking Visionary

Do you know that you go where you look? Just as a tennis player looks towards the point he wants to hit the ball, or a downhill racer looks in the direction he's skiing, your motorcycle will follow your line of sight. It sounds blindingly easy – just look where you want to go. In practice it's not that simple.

Take cornering, for example. Many riders don't look where they're going, but at the road immediately ahead. That's why they 'thruppeny bit' through bends, or turn a single change of direction into two or more changes of direction.

Looking ahead means being one step ahead. As you approach a bend you size it up, scanning as far round it as possible. Only then will you be able to determine the correct entry speed, the correct gear and when to make that single steering action. By the time you enter the corner you should be looking at your chosen apex (the point at which you stop going into the bend and start coming out), and when you reach the apex you should be looking at the exit. This is much more difficult than it sounds and comes with practice.

Using your eyes properly also means you're less likely to suffer from target fixation. Riding at night, especially in bad visibility, is a good example of target fixation; you tend to wobble through bends because you're staring at a fixed point ahead, the headlight beam.

Concentrating on your intended route means you'll corner more smoothly and it gives you time to change your line to more favourable road surfaces. But most important of all, if you face a collision, look in the direction of your escape route.

OVERTAKING

Safety Rule 1: Think Carefully Before Making A Move

Overtaking puts you in potential danger. It does so because your view ahead is likely to be obscured and the vehicle you're passing could make a manoeuvre you hadn't anticipated. Or that car, which seemed to be waiting so patiently at the junction, suddenly pulls out. Motorcycles should be the safest vehicles on which to overtake. They take up little road space, they accelerate quickly and the rider's view is usually superior to that of drivers. The fact that bikers have accidents when overtaking is often their own fault.

Let me give you an example. A motorcyclist approaches a line of cars that is slowing down, but the road ahead is perfectly clear. The biker decides to accelerate past the cars, but just as he's about to complete the manoeuvre, the car at the front turns right across his path, towards a side road. The motorcycle crashes into the side of the car. It's a common accident and it costs lives. Whenever you consider overtaking, ask yourself the following questions:

- *How have the drivers ahead been behaving up to the point I'm about to overtake?* Take extra care if you notice an erratic driver.
- *Can I see ahead well enough to overtake safely?* Don't overtake if you don't have clear vision.
- *Are there any potential hazards, like side roads?* Never overtake near a junction or other potential hazards.
- *Will my overtaking manoeuvre cause other vehicles to have to slow down to let me cut in?* Only overtake when there's plenty of clear road ahead.
- *If there's a slow-moving vehicle leading a queue of traffic, how are the cars following it going to respond?* One could impatiently pull out to overtake without warning, or the lead vehicle (often a milk float in town or tractor in the countryside) could make a sudden turn.
- *Is my speed differential too great?* Drivers of slow-moving vehicles often think and respond relatively slowly, so if you're riding too fast you might already be heading for a collision by the time the two of you have started a manoeuvre.

Safety Rule 2: Get Into The Right Position

Many motorcyclists follow directly behind the vehicle in front of them, which is exactly where they shouldn't be. First, their forward visibility will be largely obscured and, second, there will be less room for manoeuvre should the car in front brake heavily. Either in town or out on the open road, the correct following position is on the offside of the vehicle in front. This will increase your vision ahead dramatically (you can even look through the car in front) and it places you in the correct position to overtake.

Read the road ahead. Your eyes will need to continually flit between the far distance, the middle distance and whatever's directly ahead – and you'll need to interpret the changing situations. If, for example, there's a line of traffic approaching, you'll want to move towards the centre of your lane. As you come up behind another vehicle or even a line of traffic, approach the rear car on its offside. If it's clear you can overtake, pull out to start the manoeuvre before you get close to the car immediately ahead, and as you overtake move over to the far side of the road. This will give you the best possible visibility and also the greatest chance of avoiding a car that might pull out without warning.

If you've been following other vehicles and then decide you might be able to overtake, move up closer to the offside of the car ahead and select a gear that will give good acceleration. Once you've checked thoroughly behind you and indicated, and seen that the road ahead is clear, pull out. And while you're overtaking, continually look for escape routes, gaps between vehicles you may have to pull into, the speed of approaching traffic and any hazards that may be lurking behind trees or hedges.

Safety Rule 3: Watch Out For Side Roads

Some of the most common hazards in overtaking involve side roads. The golden rule of thumb is: never overtake if there is a junction ahead. You may not be able to see it (it could be obscured by a lorry) so it's important to continually read the road signs. Here are some common road situations, which often end badly for the biker:
- You are following a lorry. You pull out to overtake because the road ahead seems clear, but there's a car waiting to pull out of a hidden side road to the left. As you overtake the lorry, the car pulls out…..it

ends in disaster.
- This time you're following a lorry and there's a side road ahead to your right, with a car waiting to pull out. You see the car, hope that the driver has seen you, and start to overtake. The driver hasn't seen you and pulls out......it ends in disaster.
- You're behind a car. As you pull out to overtake, it indicates right to turn into a side road and cuts across your path......it ends in disaster.
- There's a lay-by up ahead on the left, with a car parked in it. You decide to overtake the vehicle ahead, which pulls out to let the stationary car onto the main road......it ends in disaster.

When planning to overtake, scan the road for junctions of all sorts. Farm entrances, drives to people's houses or even by-ways are all potentially dangerous, both because the car ahead may swerve to avoid a vehicle pulling out, and because a vehicle may cut across in front of you. Other places to be cautious are blind crests, humpback bridges and bends. You should also take the road condition into consideration. Spray from lorries will mean you might have to be extra-careful because visibility is reduced, or there may be potholes, diesel or damp patches you may want to avoid.

CORNERING

How Should I Steer?

Negotiating a corner should be the simplest of acts. But as any racer knows, it's also the subject of endless discussion. And for road riders it's also the cause of many accidents; most bike-only crashes happen while cornering. The trouble is that many road riders don't think about how they'll take a bend. They turn in too early, they make steering adjustments while cornering and they use the throttle jerkily - all strict No-Nos.

So how many steering changes should a rider make when taking a corner? The answer is ONE. That's the most basic rule, because it's only then that you can start riding smoothly. Even better, if you corner correctly, you can both increase your speed and your margin of safety. By making just the one steering change, as you enter the corner, the machine will settle on its suspension, you'll be able to feed in the throttle and you can start thinking about the exit.

If you enter a bend too early and run wide, one reaction is to throttle off and then throttle on, throwing the bike's weight forwards and then backwards again. First, this will alter the bike's front-to-rear weight distribution and, second, it will upset the suspension. Combined, these two factors will radically lessen tyre grip. Once you've made your single change of direction, you should then progressively get back on the throttle. Always enter a bend at a speed you know will get you through it.

What's In A Corner?

A bend is just a piece of road that curves, isn't it? To anyone interested in riding quicker or more smoothly, it's anything but. It's the essence of motorcycling; anyone can wind the throttle open in a straight line, but very few people can corner fast and safe. There are three basic points to a bend: the turn-in, the apex (the point at which you stop entering the bend and start exiting it), and the exit. It's awfully simple to get it horribly wrong - and many road riders do.

Unfortunately, the majority of bikers enter corners too early, which forces them to run wide on the exit. This can be especially dangerous in left-handers where there's oncoming traffic. Entering a bend too soon almost certainly means you'll have to make steering and throttle adjustments mid-turn, which will upset the machine. Ideally, you should make just one change of direction (at the run-in point) and then carve a perfect arc past the apex and to the exit.

One of the best ways of teaching yourself to corner smoothly is NOT to use the brakes on the entry, because then you will be both forced to correctly judge your corner speed and ride smoothly through the bend. Once you've started flowing through bends at relatively slow speeds, you can then quicken the pace.

How Fast Can I Corner?

There's an easy technique for deciding how fast you can go through a corner. It's all to do with the vanishing point. The vanishing point is the point at which the two sides of the road appear to merge. On a straight piece of road the vanishing point is a long way off, but as the road begins to turn the point becomes closer.

As you approach a bend you will begin to close up on the vanishing point. If you slow down and the vanishing point then stays at a constant distance from you, you know you can maintain your speed or even speed up slightly. However, if the vanishing point starts approaching you, then you must slow down. And when the vanishing point rushes towards you, you're in trouble!

The correct speed to maintain through a bend is when the vanishing point stays at a constant distance from you. As the road opens up and the vanishing point moves away from you, then you can accelerate.

How Should I Position The Bike?

The racing line through a bend – enter early, apex on the central white line, then drift out wide again – is fine, as long as you can see through it. But there could be unforeseen hazards, such as a slow-moving tractor or a concealed side road, so you require as much warning as possible.

The correct procedure for right-handers is: move close to the left side of the road well before you approach the bend (taking into account potholes, loose chippings, etc); brake in a straight line (if necessary); stick to the left side of the road through the bend (to gain the maximum forward visibility); and only cut in when you can see that the road ahead is clear.

The same principle applies to left-handers: move over to the central white line on the approach and follow the line through the corner until you can see the road ahead is clear, then cut in. However, here you must be aware of oncoming traffic. If there are vehicles approaching in the opposite direction, reduce your speed and move nearer to the centre of your lane.

TOWN RIDING

Survive The Cut And Thrust

The downside to riding in town is that you're very exposed. While car drivers may be the cause of most traffic fatalities, it's cyclists, pedestrians and motorcyclists who come off worst. Most crashes involving cars and motorcycles happen at junctions, and the driver – not the biker – is to blame for over 60 per cent of them. The most common accident is that of a car pulling out of a side road, into the path of the bike. Roundabouts pose another hazard for motorcyclists; they are the scene of some 20 per cent of car-bike accidents.

The trouble with towns is that they are littered with junctions, so how you approach them is vital to your well-being. The first rule is to treat every junction with caution and assume the worst. The second rule is to keep your speed reasonably close to that of other vehicles (don't travel at 40mph when everyone else is trickling along at 20mph, even if you are within the speed limit).

If there's a car waiting to pull out of a side road, don't hug the gutter. Give the driver the best chance of seeing you by staying as close to the centre of the road as possible, taking into account oncoming traffic. This will also allow you the greatest amount of reaction time if there is an emergency.

Cars often cut across lanes at roundabouts without indicating. Again, assume cars will pull out onto the roundabout and that the car on your right will cut you up as it attempts to make an early exit.

Squeezing The Most From Your Bike

There are some bikers who don't take advantage of their machines in traffic. They sit in the queues of traffic instead of filtering between the lanes, so they might as well drive a car. Filtering is perfectly legal, as long as you're riding safely, but that's up to the discretion of the police. In other words, be sensible about it and keep your speed down to a rate that allows you full control.

Although filtering may not feel safe at first, it's not the cause of many crashes. You need to keep your wits about you at all times, look well ahead and assume other drivers have not seen you. Watch out for cars changing lanes, often without indicating. As you ride along, continually assess the road ahead. Keep an eye out for vehicles pulling out of side roads (you may be hidden by traffic) and avoid erratic drivers like the plague.

Pedestrians are a hazard. People often walk out from behind tall vehicles without looking, so be extra careful near bus stops. If you are filtering past a stationary bus, it's advisable to either slow right down or stop when you reach the front of the vehicle.

Likewise, if a vehicle has stopped for no obvious reason, it could be to let a pedestrian cross the road or to let another vehicle pull out. Watch out for this, as it's very common. And finally, remember your width. Panniers and mirrors can clip cars.

Use Your Brain To Get The Upper Hand

Riding through busy traffic is largely about psychological warfare. You need to assert yourself on the road, but without taking risks. Cars will generally give you space, but if there's a particularly determined driver don't push your luck – you'll end up worse off.

RIDING THROUGH BUSY TRAFFIC IS ABOUT PSYCHOLOGICAL WARFARE

The first step is to be conspicuous, so ride with your headlight on and wear colourful clothing. For example, a bright helmet can be seen a long way off, as it sits above most traffic. This way drivers will pick you out from the very confusing and generally grey visual background. Studies on motorcycle accidents have shown that bikers who deliberately make themselves seen are less likely to be hit by other vehicles.

The second line of defence is to be physically assertive. Place your machine where it will dominate the road. So if you arrive at the front of a queue of traffic waiting at the lights, nose ahead of the leading vehicles. In addition, if you feel it's necessary, hog a whole lane to yourself – you're entitled to it.

Be cautious at traffic lights, however. It may be tempting to accelerate through amber, but you should remember many junctions are now equipped with cameras and you could be caught. Equally, don't speed off when the lights change to green. There may be another vehicle jumping amber! Have a good look before pulling away to make sure the road is clear and then accelerate away.

Finally, when you're trickling along very slowly, use the rear brake to control your speed, rather than the throttle and clutch. It's much smoother, you'll find it easier to balance and it won't put so much stress on the bike's transmission.

DISABLED BIKERS

The great news is that almost anyone can become a born-again biker. Even if you have lost a limb, or have spina bifida or MS, or are partially paralysed, you can return to biking in one form or another. Physical disability need not prevent you from accessing this passion.

The National Association for Bikers with a Disability (NABD) was set up in 1991 by a small group of people who believe that disabled people should be able to participate in motorcycling. Since then the NABD membership has grown to 2000 members.

"At first we had to fight with the authorities to achieve our aims," explains the NABD, "but now the DVLA puts people in contact with us. The most common adaptation we make to bikes is to change the hand controls, for people who have lost the use of an arm, but we also modify brake and gearchange pedals for bikers who've lost the use of a leg and we cater for others with more serious disabilities."

The NABD, which is run entirely by volunteers, is a registered charity that gives grants for motorcycle modifications and provides training to help riders return to two or three wheels. It also organises events and fund-raising activities throughout Britain, and all money raised is used to fund the adaptation grants and other services offered to disabled riders.

For more information, contact the NABD Central, Unit 16, Renrue House, Dairyhouse Lane, Dunham Massey, Altrincham, Cheshire WA14 5RD. Tel: 0161 233 0122.

TEN TOP TIPS FOR ALL BEGINNERS

1. Relax your mind and body.
2. Look well ahead.
3. If in doubt, don't do it. Don't take stupid chances.
4. Ride assertively. Use the road to your advantage.
5. Position yourself in the road where other drivers can see you best.
6. And position yourself in the road so you have maximum vision.
7. Remember, your maximum danger area is within 11 o'clock and one o'clock of your forward vision.
8. Ride smoothly and the bike will handle better.
9. Use the vanishing point to determine your speed through bends.
10. Make just one change of direction when cornering.

Chapter 12: Advanced Riding Techniques

12
Advanced Riding Techniques

"I seem to be stuck in a rut. My riding isn't improving. I think I've got a good feel for the bike, but I don't know how to broaden my ability. It's frustrating, because I know I can do better, and I'm still making silly mistakes. The worst thing is my mates are leaving me behind."
Jim, 47 years.

Many riders reach a certain level of ability and then stop learning. It could be because they've become complacent, or that they've stopped thinking about what they're doing, or that they simply don't have the knowledge. It doesn't matter who you are, or how good you think you are, you can always improve on your riding. Even world champions want to learn more, because there's always someone else willing to push it that little bit further. Honing your skills just takes an inquisitive mind.

PART 1: AT ONE WITH YOUR BIKE

Think With Your Backside

When you ride a motorcycle, you should think through your backside. It's all too easy to sit there like a stiff old clod, ignorant of what the machine's telling you. Your bottom is one of your main contact points with the machine and it can relay masses of information to you. That means being sensitive to it. Your backside has to work hard. It can tell you how the suspension is working, how well the tyres are gripping, how much throttle to use and how your bike is reacting under braking.

The first rule is to relax. Let your arms go floppy, let your shoulders droop, and keep your legs and back supple. Then you can start riding through the seat of your pants, which is doubly important to do in the wet, as the contact patches between your tyres and the road are small.

When you power out of corners you should feel for grip at the back tyre. Forget about the front because the stresses are now being put through the rear, which is the most likely end to slide. Your backside should also tell you what the weight distribution is of your bike when you corner. Ideally the front should be lighter than the rear, which is achieved when the throttle is rolled on immediately the machine has turned. And your posterior should also be sensing how well the suspension is working, which in turn lets you know how much throttle or brake to apply.

Of course different types of bikes feed back varying degrees of information to the rider (a well set-up sports bike will provide its pilot with a detailed account of what it's doing, while at the opposite end of the spectrum the custom bike gives little away). But whichever type of motorcycle you ride, you should communicate with it through your bum.

THINK WITH YOUR BACKSIDE

Body Language Is An Art

The first thing most riders do when they brake hard is to sit up. It's actually wrong, because the combined centre of gravity of man and machine is then positioned higher and further forward, making it easier for the rear wheel to become airborne. Much of the art of motorcycling is about where, and when, you move your body.

A human's centre of gravity is at mid-chest height, so generally this should be kept as low as possible on the bike. Thus when you sit up to brake, too much weight is thrown over the front of the motorcycle.

If you have to perform an emergency stop in the dry, you're best off gripping the fuel tank with your knees, pushing your bum back, and keeping your torso low. When the road is dry tyre grip is not an issue, while the prone position helps keep the rear wheel on the ground.

However, if the road surface is wet, you'll want as much grip from the front tyre as possible. In addition, you won't be able to brake so hard that the rear of the bike lifts, so you sit up and brace yourself on the handlebars. This will force weight onto the tyre, giving it the extra adhesion it needs.

Similarly, if you accelerate hard, don't sit there like a stuffed pudding. Move yourself forward, which keeps the weight over the front of the machine to stop it lifting. Modern, high-powered bikes wheelie with ease in both first and second gears, so weight transfer is important in the low gears.

Controlling The Throttle

Learn throttle control and you've mastered half the art of smooth riding. If you're not greedy with the throttle, you'll be able to control your machine better. This is especially true in the wet. Jerky throttle movements cause the bike to become unstable, which affects tyre grip. Whacking the throttle open can cause the rear wheel to spin or lift the front wheel off the ground, while chopping the throttle hard in a bend can result in the front tyre sliding.

You have to be sensitive to your machine's ability, but you also need good observation, anticipation and judgement of speed and distance. For example, if you accelerate hard you might find you have to use the brakes excessively because you've caught up with the traffic ahead too quickly. Being over-enthusiastic with the gas doesn't mean you'll cover ground faster.

Good throttle control is crucial to good cornering. Most road riders are lazy with their throttle, waiting till they are two-thirds of the way through a corner before they roll it on. As soon as a bike starts cornering, it begins to lose speed, putting undue stress on the front tyre. Ideally your machine should have a 60-40 per cent rear-to-front weight distribution, which gives the greatest range of suspension movement and best grip by the front tyre.

To achieve this in a turn, you need to wind on the throttle smoothly and consistently as soon as possible once your bike has completed its change of direction. And as the turn opens up, you can start accelerating away.

Be A Smooth Operator

Suspension determines how you ride a motorcycle. And how your suspension works depends on how aggressive you are with the throttle. If you want ultimate grip from your tyres, you need the suspension to work at its optimum, which means you must operate the throttle smoothly.

Forks or shocks which have used their full extension of travel will put enormous pressure on the tyres, because the wheels won't be able to move up and down quickly enough to follow the contours of the road. When you're hard on the brakes, the front end feels heavy and steering is sluggish, while when you accelerate quickly the front goes light and the handlebars can shake violently. Similarly, fully-extended suspension will not give good feedback.

Ideally you should keep your suspension mid-way through the first third of its travel. By being smooth with the throttle, the forks and shock operate most efficiently. Riders who are on-off the gas are asking their suspension to compensate for the huge weight transfers generated by the machine pitching back and forth. With the combined weight of rider and bike, small throttle adjustments can effectively transfer 150lbs one way or the other.

Of course the suspension on many bikes is adjustable, but the throttle is the key to its set-up. If you run into a corner fast and off the throttle, you'll use up precious fork travel that should be used to keep the front tyre in contact with the road. Similarly, if you power out of bends too hard the shock will become less compliant, putting undue stress on the rear tyre. For best results, you should roll on the gas smoothly and evenly as you go through a bend.

PART 2: BRAKING

Take A Break From Braking

Hard braking is one of the most heart-stopping moments on a bike. It takes up a huge amount of concentration, saps energy and stops you thinking about your next move. It's almost as if your brain comes to a halt with the bike. Which is why you should try riding without the brakes.

American race instructor Keith Code gets his pupils to ride the track without using their brakes at all. Instead of their minds becoming overloaded with having to slow down for corners, they can concentrate on the important aspects of riding, like throttle control and cornering speeds.

Code's tactic definitely works, and is well worth trying on the road. When you next go for a ride, stay off the brakes unless it's absolutely necessary. For a start, when you approach a corner you'll find that it's easier to judge the bend and your correct entry speed. With just a little practice you'll actually start cornering quicker.

The second reward is that your throttle control will improve massively. Where you previously charged up to a bend or a vehicle in front and had to hit the brakes, you now think about what you're doing with your right wrist. Your anticipation improves and you learn to use the engine for both accelerating and slowing down. Finally, by not using the brakes you become a smoother and faster rider. No longer do you hammer up to a bend, slam on the anchors, tip the machine in hard and then wind on the gas. Now you flow, which is the secret to good riding.

Front Brake Good, Rear Brake Bad

I once saw a totally unnecessary accident – which was potentially deadly – at a race meeting. A rider had approached a hairpin, slammed on both front and rear brakes, the back wheel locked up and he was spat off his machine, breaking a collarbone in the process. Is it necessary to use the rear brake?

The physics of braking say "no". When you apply the front brake hard, the motorcycle's weight is thrown forward, the forks compress and the rear wheel either goes light or comes off the ground. If the rear wheel stops spinning, most of the motorcycle's stability from the headstock back is lost. And when the locked-up rear wheel lands, it will simply skid along the ground.

With the exception of custom and trail bikes, there's no advantage to using the back brake. If you need convincing, try stopping from 30mph with just the rear and see how long it takes. Forever. And that's if you manage not to lock up the wheel. Then repeat the experiment using just the front brake - and see the dramatic difference. There are two exceptions to the front brake-only rule: use both brakes, either if the road is damp or if you are carrying a passenger, but even then be careful. The simple fact is that the front can do 100 per cent of the work.

Ease On The Brakes For Harder Stopping

There are numerous ways to use a bike's front brake when entering a corner: pull the lever and maintain a constant pressure; pull hard at first and then ease off; pull gently at first and then increase the pressure; or go light, hard and then light again. Which is best?

Remember that the bike's weight will be thrown onto the front wheel under braking, which compresses the forks. If you hit the brake too hard initially, the forks are liable to bottom out and the front tyre could then lose traction. In addition, as more force is transferred through the front of the motorcycle, the heavier the steering will become.

The correct procedure is first to apply moderate pressure to the lever, let the forks settle, then apply the brakes hard, and finally ease off as you approach the bend. Ideally you should be completely off the brakes when you enter the turn, allowing the bike's suspension to settle before you make the change of direction.

Braking deep into a corner can be dangerous, especially in left-handers. It slows down steering and loads up the front tyre when it has the least grip, and is the cause of numerous fatalities (the front washes out and you can slam into oncoming traffic). If you need to brake in a corner, the only way to do so is to gradually increase pressure on the lever as you stand the machine up. You'll almost certainly crash if you try to brake hard while remaining cranked over.

Brake Hard, Turn Quick

Now for some fun. If you want to make your bike turn really quickly, do so with the brakes. When you apply the front brake, the forks compress and the machine tends to stand on its nose, which effectively gives it a steeper steering angle. Use this to your advantage. The trick is to brake reasonably hard and make your change of direction as you let the front brake off. The forks will remain compressed into the turn, because the front end is loaded with the force of cornering. Once the machine is cranked over, the suspension settles and you can get back on the throttle.

Do this enough and you'll soon discover that you can go from letting off the brake to accelerating very quickly. You'll also find that because the bike turns quicker, you can enter corners later and more accurately. Don't start off by being too aggressive. First get a feel for what the motorcycle is doing and as your confidence builds up you can begin to push it harder.

The best place to practise is on a race track, where you can pick one particular bend (preferably a slow to medium speed one) and attack it with increasing enthusiasm. Unless you are completely overdoing it, the front wheel will not wash out. Get it right and you'll sharpen up your riding no end. But for heaven's sake don't brake-and-turn in the wet!

PART 3: COUNTER STEERING

Turn Left To Go Right!

I remember when I first heard about counter steering. I could hardly believe it. Pull on the left bar to turn right? Pull on the right bar to turn left? What? Then I tried it – and it was like discovering the meaning of life. It transformed my riding. Suddenly I could make my bike turn quickly and accurately. Many road riders simply use their body weight to tip their bike onto its side to make it corner, which is both cumbersome and imprecise.

To understand counter steering, you should know a bit about your bike's mechanics. The wheels of a motorcycle act as two gyroscopes, and while the bike is travelling in a straight line it's normally very stable. The faster you go, the greater the gyroscopic force of the wheels, so the more difficult it is to turn the machine. Cornering is about beating that gyroscopic effect.

Now if you want to counter steer to turn right, for example, you pull on the left bar (or push on the right), which points the wheel in the opposite direction to the one you intend going. The machine then leans over onto the right-hand curved profile of the tyres, making the bike turn to the right. Likewise, if you pull/push the bars in the opposite direction, the motorcycle will turn left.

REMEMBER – PULL LEFT TO GO RIGHT AND PULL RIGHT TO GO LEFT!

PULL LEFT...

...TO GO RIGHT

COUNTER STEERING'S EASY

The more you pull/push the bars, the more your bike will lean and the tighter it will steer. People's first fear about counter steering is that the front tyre will lose grip, and they'll crash. Of course, if you yank really hard on the bars this could happen, but you'd have to be extremely ham-fisted to do this.

But counter steering does take time to get used to. If you're feeling nervous about pulling on the handlebars the 'wrong' way, start off slowly and build up. First, ride along a straight piece of road and pull gently on the right bar. You'll find your bike moves to the left. And when you pull on the left bar, your bike will move to the right. Magic!

Now go to a bend you know well and try counter steering. Suddenly, your bike is no longer the cuddly, cumbersome object you love so much, but a surgical instrument which can corner with pinpoint precision. You'll discover that even minute pressure on the bars is enough to make a change of direction.

Very soon you'll find that you can be quite brutal with the bars without upsetting the machine's stability, but the faster you turn, the more accurate you need to be. To get round a corner quickly and safely, you should then start thinking about where you turn your bike, how quickly you turn it, and what angle of lean you need.

PART 4: LEAN MACHINE

Know Your Limit

Leaning a bike over is part of everyday life for the motorcyclist. Each time you negotiate a corner you have to lean the machine into the bend, although for some it doesn't come easy. There are so many factors involved riders often find it too daunting to get anywhere near the limit. But if you enter a bend too fast (and we've all done it at some time) you'll run wide unless you have a sufficient angle of lean. This can be extremely dangerous, especially in left-hand corners where there might be oncoming traffic.

Here are the variables you must consider:

- Tyres: The most common problem is lack of faith in the tyres. People think the rubber will lose grip if the bike is leant too far over. The fact is that most modern tyres will cope with the maximum lean angle of the machine, as long as the road is dry and reasonably grippy, and you're riding smoothly.
- Road Surface: This is crucial to tyre grip. If it's damp or covered in gravel, for example, then obviously the angle of lean will be restricted. You should be continually assessing the Tarmac you're riding and should have a good idea – before you enter a bend – as to how grippy it is. If you're uncertain, slow down.
- Suspension: Your machine's suspension set-up will partly determine the motorcycle's maximum angle of lean. As you go through a bend, the bike's suspension compresses, so softly-suspended machines have less ground clearance than firmly-suspended ones. The former also tend to bounce more over bumps, which can cause parts like the footpegs to dig into the road surface.
- On Or Off: Whether you lean off your bike or not makes a big difference. Road riders tend not to move their body weight to the inside of a bend, but doing so actually helps keep the bike more upright.

How To Learn How To Lean

Crazy lean angles may look impressive on the race track, but do it on the road and you're asking for trouble. However, you should know how far you can push your bike – it could save your life if you enter a corner too quickly.

Ideally, you should find an empty car park and ride in circles, leaning further over bit by bit. This simply isn't an option for most people. Or you could use a roundabout, but the police wouldn't be too happy about it. More easily, you could attend a track day and concentrate on one corner (preferably a slow one).

The alternative is to rely on experience. The more you ride and the more used you become to your motorcycle, the better you will understand its machinations. If you ride a route regularly, pick a safe, well-surfaced corner with a constant radius and positive camber, and each time you negotiate it, go through a little quicker, but look out for the bike's warning signs that leaning is not going according to plan:

- The machine becomes choppy or bouncy. When that happens, slow down. The suspension is having difficulty coping.
- You hear a scraping noise. The first part of a bike to touch down is usually the footpeg, when you'll hear a metallic scraping noise. Footpegs are normally hinged, so they have some 'give'. If you continue to push it and a fixed part of the bike touches the deck, it could lift a wheel and you'll crash.
- The rear tyre slides a little. The bike will wiggle suddenly when this happens and it's time to back off.

The bottom line is never to corner faster than either you or your machine are capable of, but if you're going to overshoot a bend, lean the machine as far over as necessary to get round it. At least if you crash then, you've given yourself every chance.

Steer With Your Weight

When you steer a motorcycle, you can effectively redistribute your body weight, thus making it easier for the bike to turn. You can make your bike think the centre of gravity is low, even though you're still on top of the machine.

When you're firmly seated, with hands clasping the 'bars, feet lightly positioned on the 'pegs and your belly on the tank, your bulk does nothing to help change the bike's direction. Rather, it hinders it.

But there is a solution, which involves some physical effort. By placing your weight on the footpegs in a turn, you take your weight off the seat and transfer it to a lower part of the machine. A motorcycle rotates around its centre of gravity, so the nearer your body weight is to the centre of that mass, the easier it is for it to turn.

There are two schools of thought about how you place your weight on the footpegs. Some riders place most of their weight on the inside 'peg; the theory is that it pushes down the inside of the machine, making it steer quicker. However, the rider is then placing his weight on the least stable place.

The other, more cogent school says you should place your weight on the outer 'peg. As your weight is effectively near to the bike's centre of gravity and the wheels are acting as gyroscopes, doing this doesn't make the machine stand up. It has an added advantage as it helps push your body weight to the inside of the corner as well.

Weighting the outside 'peg also helps stabilise the machine through a bend. Gravity is pulling the bike to the outside, so any bounce or loss of grip will cause the tyres to slide in that direction too. By pushing down on the outer footpeg, you'll help prevent unwanted slides, which is especially helpful in slippery conditions.

How To Get Your Knee Down

Most motorcyclists are fascinated by knee-down action. I've yet to meet a biker who isn't thrilled by the cornering antics of racers, when their knee sliders scrape the Tarmac as they lean their machines over. For road riders, getting their knee down for the first time is one of life's great thrills. If you're thinking of taking part in a track day, it's a technique well worth learning. It takes practice and confidence, but it's surprisingly easy to master. Here's how to do it:

First, relax. You want your body to be as supple as possible, to flow with the bike as it goes over the bumps. If you're rigid, you will bob up and down on the machine and upset the suspension. Lean forward and point your shoulder in the direction you intend turning.

Second, place the balls of your feet on the footpegs and lift your weight off the seat (like a jockey). This has two advantages: your legs act as secondary shock absorbers; and by placing all your weight directly on to the pegs, the combined centre of gravity of you and your bike is lowered.

Then, as you approach the corner and before you brake, slide your backside over the seat so the cheek nearest the inside of the corner hangs off the machine. As you do this, stick your knee out at roughly 45 degrees.

Next comes the more difficult bit. You have to corner at a speed which allows the bike to lean over sufficiently for your knee slider to scrape the ground.

Your Knee Is A Gauge

Getting your knee down may look great, but it's also extremely useful. And with so many people taking part in track days now, it's worth knowing why it works. I've already explained that it moves the combined centre of gravity - of rider and motorcycle - to the inside of the corner, so keeping the machine more upright; it counters the centrifugal forces of the wheels; and it's a great psychological help.

The immediate benefit is that once you start getting your knee down, you'll then know exactly how far you're leaning the bike in a bend. As long as your body is in the same position each turn, your knee becomes an accurate gauge. If on a race circuit your knee just touches the Tarmac through a particular corner, and the bike remains steady, you'll know you can go through that bend a little faster the next lap.

The second advantage is that when your knee is pointed out, it creates wind resistance in the direction you wish to turn - and it's far easier to flick the bike over when there's a drag to that side.

The third advantage is that when your knee is touching the Tarmac as you corner, you don't have so far to fall! I once lost the front end of my bike at over 100mph when I had my knee down and slid graciously to a halt (only my pride was hurt).

And finally, if you're a master of the technique, you can save a crash by propping the machine up on your knee as the tyres begin to lose grip. If that sounds far-fetched, four-times grand prix champion Eddie Lawson claims he used to do it at least once a lap.

PART 5: SCRATCHING

Feast Your Eyes On The Country!

We all love going out for a blast on a summer's day. There's nothing more exhilarating than scything down twisty roads, getting a whiff of those country smells and flowing with the rhythm of the bike. It's moments like these that make motorcycling so special. Of course part of the enjoyment is the huge variety of challenges we face – and getting them right. Hump-back bridges, blind hills, blind bends and different types of corners only add to the pleasure.

Here your most important instruments are your eyes. You not only need to look where you're going, but you also have to interpret the road ahead. Many bikers fail this first hurdle because they don't build up the visual skills necessary to ride smoothly. You tend to go where you look. In the same way as tennis players look at where they want the ball to land, you should be looking at where you want you and your bike to go (as well as scanning the road for possible dangers).

The next step is to rid yourself of target fixation. If your attention is completely absorbed by a car waiting to pull out of a side road, for example, you won't be prepared for other dangers that may be developing in the meantime. Finally you need to scan the road ahead – not a few feet ahead, but as far down the road as the eye can see. As your speed increases, your visual skill becomes ever more critical. If you combine these visual skills, you'll be amazed by the results.

Cutting Corners Is Your Right

As you use your eyes more effectively, you naturally build up confidence and ride smoother, faster and safer. That country lane blast is now even more enjoyable. It's time to take some short cuts – literally. The road is there for you to use, so unless markings and signs tell you otherwise, make full use of it. Ideally (traffic permitting) you should turn each bend into the straightest line possible. That's not to say you should recklessly cut through blind corners.

The conventional way to approach a right-hand bend, for example, is to stick close to the left side of the road, follow the curvature of the corner and cut in when you see the road ahead is clear. When you can see through the right-hander before you even reach it, you can take a far more radical line.

On tight, bendy roads where the view ahead is clear, you still approach the corner on the left side of the road, but then cut in much earlier and make your apex on the far side of the road. In other words, you cut the corner, which enables you to take a smoother and faster line.

Similarly, you're perfectly entitled to straight-line through a series of zig-zag bends, watching the road move from side to side as you maintain a constant line. Some people find that straight-lining corners goes against the grain, but that's because they're not looking far enough ahead. If you intend using the full width of the road, you need to be sure there's nothing coming the other way.

Look Out!

Traffic-free country roads may be a laugh when everything's going smoothly, but they are also littered with dangerous obstacles that can catch you out. One moment you're grinning from ear to ear, the next thing you know is someone's applying the elastoplast.

Here are some of the more common hazards, and how you should deal with them when they occur:

- Blind Corner: If the road's traffic-free and well-surfaced, it's tempting to stay on the pace through a blind bend. This is a bad idea. The road surface may change suddenly, there could be an entrance to a field on the corner, or there may be a slow-moving vehicle ahead of you. Slow down to a speed from which you could stop in an emergency.
- Partially Blind Corner: You can see into the bend, but hedges obscure the apex. For all the above reasons, don't take the chance. During those lovely summer months, slow-moving tractors will be active, so also expect clumps of dried mud lying on the Tarmac. Again, slow down.
- Hidden Side Road: Entrances to fields and small side roads are often obscured by high hedgerows, so you can easily fail to notice them until it's too late. And because visibility is bad for the driver pulling out as well, keep an eye out for them – and slow right down if a bonnet protrudes from the bushes!
- Hump-Back Bridge: Some hump-back bridges are far more acute than they appear so, if you don't want to become airborne, approach

them slowly and with great caution.
- Blind Rise: This is also known as 'dead man's hill'. Unless you want to bury yourself in the back of a lorry, always slow down to a speed at which you can stop. The more acute the rise, the more you should slow down.
- Tractor: Even if you can see a tractor ahead, your brain might not be tuned into the speed differential between you and it – with the result that you have to heave on the anchors to avoid running up the back of it. Tractor drivers also have an annoying habit of turning when you least expect them to – and often without signalling.
- Line Of Cars: There are several cars ahead, moving very slowly. You decide to accelerate past. Just as you do so the lead car turns right, across your path. You've made two potentially fatal errors: you haven't read the road and your overtaking speed was too great.

PART 6: WHAT TO DO WHEN......

......You Lose The Front End

I was braking for a junction when, for no apparent reason, the front wheel of my bike locked up. As I released the brake lever I saw a flattened plastic drinks bottle flick up from under the tyre! However, you're far more likely to lock up your front wheel on diesel or in the wet. If you panic and continue to grip the lever, the front end will 'tuck under' and you'll crash.

But losing the front end can also happen when the roads are dry. All it takes is a patch of loose chippings, or an over-enthusiastic grab at the brake lever, to lock up the front wheel. The solution, obviously, is to let go of the lever as soon as you feel the front end going and, when the machine has righted itself, re-apply the brake. Your reaction has to be lightning-quick and you need to stay composed enough to work out what to do next.

You can teach yourself how to do this by riding at about 30mph in a straight line, on a clear road, and grabbing the brake lever for an instant to make the tyre squeal. You may need a few attempts to build up your confidence, but once you've succeeded you'll be prepared for a real emergency. And you can help prevent the front wheel locking up in the first place by squeezing the brake lever progressively, which will give you greater feel for what the front tyre is doing.

......You Go Into A Corner Too Fast

The rise in solo bike accidents is chiefly down to one factor, according to the police: motorcyclists approach corners too fast, believe they can't get round, panic and run off the road. It's such a common problem with born-again bikers that the main insurance companies have imposed stinging premiums on people wanting to insure powerful sportsters like Yamaha's R1, Honda's FireBlade and Kawasaki's ZX-9R.

These superbikes are deceptively fast, leading many people straight into trouble. Some riders simply don't realise how quickly they're approaching bends – until it's too late – while others believe their machines will let them get away with anything. In both cases people are riding beyond their ability.

If you do find yourself entering a corner too quickly, your only hope is to:

1. Remain calm. If you panic you'll certainly become another statistic.
2. Lean the bike into the bend. You'll be surprised how far a sports bike can lean in the right conditions, so take advantage.
3. If you're agile enough – and have the presence of mind – you should also move your body towards the inside of the corner. This will effectively shift the combined centre of gravity (of you and your bike) towards the outside of the bend, so keeping the machine more upright.
4. As a last resort you can also gently apply the brakes to scrub off a little speed, although this carries the risk of a wheel locking up and sliding. Whatever you do, don't grab at the brake lever, as the front wheel will lock up.

......You Suddenly Get A Tank Slapper

Beware of the dreaded tank slapper on your country lane blast. Many people assume they only happen on sports bikes with radical steering geometry, but they can also happen on very conservative machines.

Tank slappers are frightening. The handlebars swing uncontrollably from side to side. A moderate slapper may be no more than a slight wiggle of the front wheel, but a bad one has the forks banging from lock to lock.

Modern sports bikes are particularly prone to slappers, because of their radical steering geometry. Their front wheel acts like the wheels of a shopping trolley, trying to spin round, and is thus prone to instability when the front of the bike becomes light. But traditionally-styled machines suffer because the back of the bike is low, so under acceleration the rear suspension becomes compressed and the front wheel becomes too light. All that's needed then is a slight bump to make the front wheel slap.

You can usually control a tank slapper, but you'll have to keep your nerve. The normal reaction is to panic, shut the throttle and sit up - just the opposite of what you ought to do. The best (and only) solution is to lean forward and maintain a constant throttle. If the tank slapper persists, you should then attempt to power out of it, although you'll have to react quickly.

......You Quickly Need To Alter The Angle Of Lean

It's easy to get carried away when you go out for a spin - and you can get into serious trouble if you start cornering enthusiastically. Modern machines and tyres are capable of extreme lean angles, so grounding out parts of the bike can happen without warning.

The first sign that you're near the limit is when a footpeg scrapes the Tarmac, but footpegs are spring-loaded, so when the 'hero blob' hits the road the peg will be forced up. However, if you push the bike too hard the exhaust or frame may touch the ground. When a solid part, such as the silencer, touches down the rear wheel can lift and you'll crash (unless you're very lucky).

The problem is compounded on bumpy roads, especially on bikes with soft suspension. You may enter a corner at a speed you consider reasonable, only to find that your bike wallows over bumps, the suspension compresses and you suddenly lose vital ground clearance.

There are two ways to solve the problem. The first is to ride slower. Experience and knowledge of your bike's behaviour under different conditions will tell you how far you can lean over. If you've reached the stage where your bike is grounding out regularly, you're an accident waiting to happen.

The second solution is to hang off the bike. By leaning your body into the bend you'll be able keep your machine more upright, as you will have moved the bike's centre of gravity outwards – and the more you lean your body into the bend, the more upright you'll keep the bike.

TEN TOP TIPS FOR ALL ADVANCED RIDERS

1. Always ride within your ability.
2. Use your body – it's an integral part of the bike.
3. Learn how to lean off.
4. Improve your forward vision.
5. Practise riding without the brakes.
6. Learn how to counter steer.
7. Use the throttle smoothly.
8. Use as much of the road as possible.
9. Continually re-assess your riding.
10. Never become complacent.

Chapter 13: Tuning Your Bike

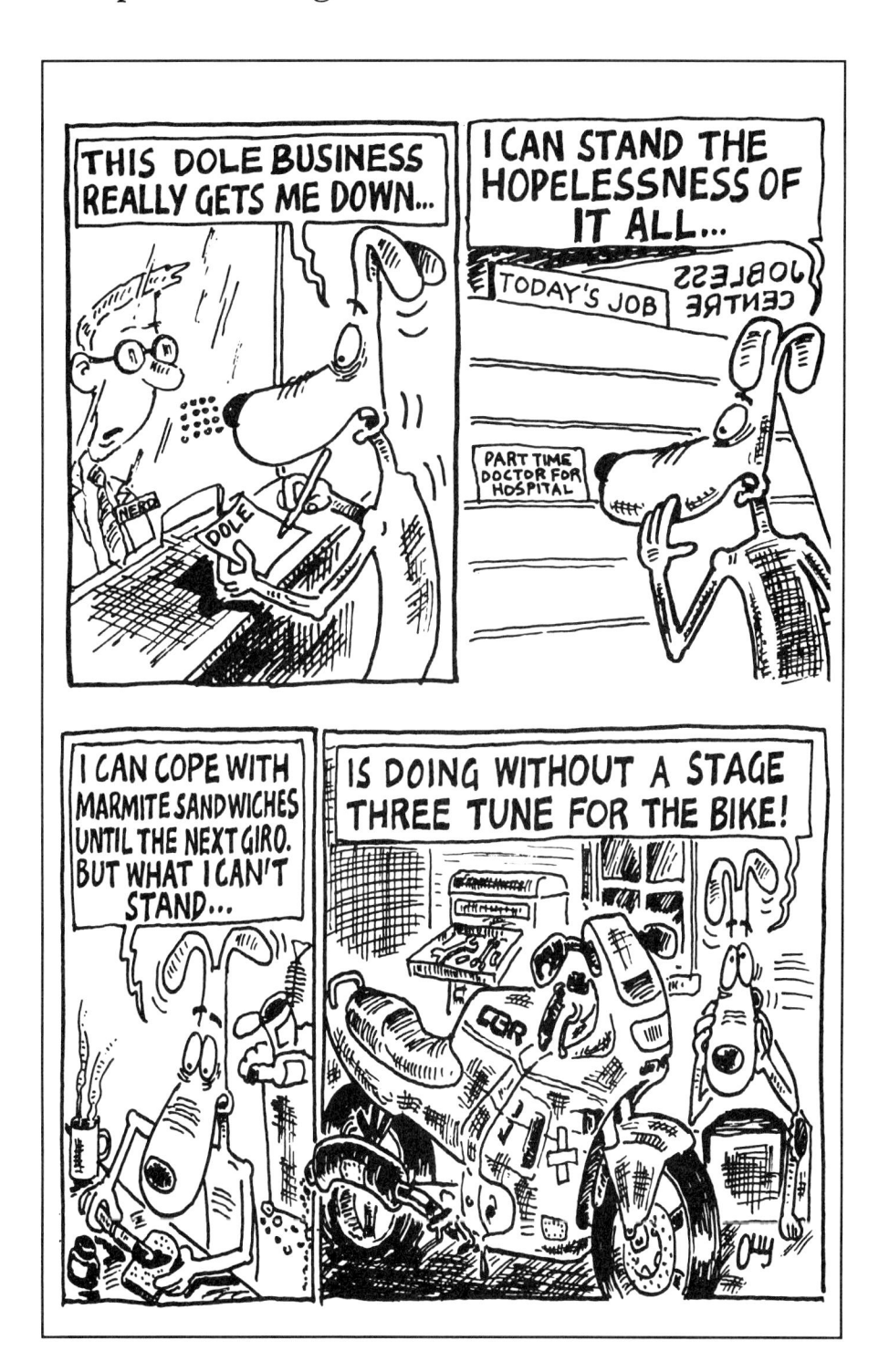

13
Tuning Your Bike

"My motorcycle has multi-adjustable suspension. A mate fiddled with it and now the bike feels really odd – and I haven't a clue how to sort it out. I'm also getting to the point where I'd like to change my bike, but I feel an engine tune would give it a new lease of life. What should I do?"
Eddie, 34 years.

Tuning your bike is loads of fun. You can alter the way it handles by sorting the suspension, you can tweak the engine so it goes faster and sounds better, while a different set of tyres can alter the way it handles. For a little over £1000 you can make such drastic changes to your bike that it feels like a different machine; for many riders, this is a worthwhile expense. The thrill of collecting your bike after it has been tuned is a revelation. Enjoy!

The Bouncy Bits

Suspension, to most people, is a black art. If you own a bike with some degree of sporty pretension, the forks and shock will almost certainly be adjustable to some degree. The factories set these to cater for most of the riders for most of the time. However, you may feel the settings don't suit you. You may find that while they work well enough on the road, the bike starts to wallow when you're riding fast on the track, or that the forks bottom out under braking. Inevitably you set to work, probably make it worse, and end up stuck down a blind alley.

Let's start from scratch. First, you need to know what's what:
<u>Monoshock</u> This is the single shock that's fitted to most modern bikes, normally between the engine and rear wheel. Its advantage over twin shocks is that its internal components are bigger and so can move more oil, which is crucial for good damping. Mono units generally contain

high-pressure gas, which keeps the oil stable in the unit.

<u>Twin Shocks</u> These are placed between the frame and the swingarm, so theoretically react instantly to movements of the swingarm. However, they are smaller than mono units, so the compression damping rod is smaller-diameter and therefore moves less oil. Many less sporty bikes still have twin shocks, but this is mainly for styling.

<u>Telescopic Forks</u> These are the long, tube-like things at the front of the bike, which come in two types – conventional and upside-down. The advantage of conventional forks is that they are generally 3.5kg lighter than upside-down units; the advantage of upside-down forks is that they are more rigid and the wheel carries less unsprung weight. Although they look different externally, internally they are the same. Upside-down forks are currently in fashion on sports bikes, but there's no way you'd be able to tell the two apart while riding on the road.

The suspension's job is to provide good ride quality, keep the tyres in contact with the road, and to maintain the bike's stability. If you've ever ridden a rigid rear-end bike, or one with a plunger-type rear end, you'll understand why suspension is so crucial, and why sprung saddles used to be the order of the day!

How To Set Up The Forks

Some forks aren't adjustable (in which case you can't twiddle them), others have adjustable spring preload only, and yet others have adjustable preload and rebound and/or compression damping. The range of adjustability on most road bikes is limited and the factory settings are generally reasonably correct. However, there is some leeway, which can make a difference.

If you are going to reset the suspension of your bike, read the manual and make sure you set both forks to the same settings. Set the spring preload first and then work on the rebound and compression damping, one at a time.

- **Spring Preload** The preload adjuster acts on the springs and the preload adjusting nut sits on the top of the fork. Ideally you want the front of the bike to sag about 20 to 25mm (sag is the difference between the forks' full extension and the bike at rest on the suspension). This is achieved by winding the preload adjuster in or out. To check the sag, lift the front of the bike and then see how far it drops before it comes to a rest. The springs on many bikes are so soft that, even if you wind the preload in fully, you will not achieve the desired sag. Compressing the springs doesn't make them harder. All it does is lift up the front of the bike, which provides more fork travel and gives it a less acute steering geometry. For example, if you increase the preload because the forks bottom out under braking, the fork travel is greater and thus the forks are less likely to bottom out.

- **Rebound Damping** This controls the rate at which the suspension extends after it has been compressed. The rebound adjusting screw protrudes from the top of both the conventional and upside-down forks. Rebound damping is crucial to a bike's handling, as it works against the spring by tempering the rate at which it rebounds. The damping should normally be set mid-position, about 1 to 1.5 turns from maximum (fully wound in), although some bikes will need the damping set nearer to maximum.
- **Compression Damping** This slows down the rate at which the spring compresses when the wheel hits a bump, or when the rider brakes hard. The compression adjusting screw is placed at the bottom of the fork leg. As compression damping works in conjunction with the spring, its value is far lower than rebound damping, and it should be set as soft as possible. To find the ideal setting for your bike, start with the compression fully wound out (anticlockwise), go for a ride over bumpy roads and brake hard. Then wind the screw in half a turn at a time, trying the bike out, until you find the optimum setting. Too much compression damping could make the forks feel very harsh, and the front tyre could then lose adhesion when cornering hard.

How To Deal With A Monoshock

Use the following guidelines to help you:
- **Spring Preload** The preload setting should allow for 5 to 10mm of sag at the rear of the bike. The spring preload adjuster is normally a collar-type, and you'll need a special C-spanner (usually included in the bike's tool kit) to wind the collar up or down; winding the collar down increases the preload, winding it up does the reverse. Limited space around the shock often means that adjusting the preload is a right pain, and in some cases impossible. You may have to increase the preload if you are carrying a pillion. As with the forks, increasing

the preload does not make the spring stiffer, but simply lifts the back of the bike up, giving the shock greater travel.
- **Rebound Damping** The adjuster is always positioned at the bottom of the shock and is either a knurled knob or a slotted screw. Maximum adjustment is set by winding the knob or screw in clockwise. Average settings for road riding are 10 clicks off maximum for the knob-type and 1 to 1.5 turns off maximum for the screw-type. If the rear of your bike wallows, try increasing the rebound damping.
- **Compression Damping** The adjuster is normally a screw-type, located on the remote gas cylinder located away from the shock, and should be set mid-position on most bikes. If the damping is set high, the rear of the bike will feel harsh.

Tuning Your Suspension

When most people decide to tune their bike, they opt for an engine tune, which is expensive. While a tuned motor may provide extra power, it won't help you ride faster and it certainly won't cure any of your bike's handling problems. There's another and far less expensive way of increasing your machine's performance: get the suspension tuned.

The irony is that, while most bikes are plenty quick enough, the suspension on virtually all can be improved. It's easy for manufacturers to cut corners in suspension, because the internal workings cannot be seen and, anyway, the settings will supposedly be acceptable to the average road rider. However, tuned suspension completely changes the way your bike steers, tracts through bends and copes with road bumps.

An evil-handling, wallowy machine can be transformed into a surgically-sharp instrument, a budget bike can be made to feel like a finely-honed racer. And, of course, the better-handling your bike, the more confidence you'll have in its ability to go fast. In any case, the art of motorcycling is about how competently you corner, not how fast you can go in a straight line. Tuned suspension gives you the ability to ride faster, a tuned engine does not.

The suspension expert will respring and revalve your forks to suit your bike, which costs around £160. In some cases he will be able to rebuild the standard shock, which costs about £80; otherwise you will have to buy an aftermarket unit, ranging in price from £200 to £600.

Getting The Most From Your Engine

What a buzz! You've just picked your bike up from the tuner and it instantly feels more responsive. And when the power cuts in, it does so with a bang. Your tired old motor now has real get-up-and-go.

There are various options you can go for, depending on what you want from your bike. The engine can be tweaked for greater mid-range power, a greater top-end rush, or you can simply fit a race-style end can. Don't forget, however, that most tune-ups will simply rob power from one area of the rev range and move it to another.

Noise, Luvverly Noise

The majority of people spend their money on aftermarket silencers – and who can blame them? Even though many end cans are illegally loud, they sound great and certainly make your bike feel faster. A race-style can may liberate a few more horsepower, as it will allow the exhaust to breathe more freely, but the improvement will be negligible.

If you do fit a race silencer, don't forget that it exceeds the 82 decibel noise limit, will not pass an MoT, and that you may be picked up by the police – which won't exactly make your day. You should also check directly with the manufacturer to find out whether the carburettors need rejetting.

Beefing Up The Mid-Range

The majority of road riders (and many racers) benefit most from increasing the mid-range power of their bikes. Greater mid-range makes the engine more tractable and so easier to drive, and is especially useful when you need to power out of corners or want to overtake other traffic.

This is commonly known as the Stage One tune, which entails gas-flowing the cylinder head (which allows the gasses to flow more freely), increasing the compression ratio (by skimming the cylinder head or barrel to make the cylinder volume smaller) and dialling in the cams (to make sure the valves open and close at exactly the right time). The Stage One tune will not necessarily improve top-end performance. The engine work costs in the region of £600 and an aftermarket silencer is about £200.

Finding That Adrenaline Buzz

While a Stage One tune is useful, a Stage Two jobbie can result in eye-popping, top-end performance. Because it normally robs the motor of mid-range traction, when the power does cut in it does so with arm-wrenching gusto. The problem with a Stage Two tune is that it makes your bike more difficult to ride, and on the road you're certainly better off with greater torque.

The work includes everything that is carried out for a Stage One tune, plus crank balancing, blueprinting, and perhaps lighter pistons and different cams. Here you're looking at a £1500 bill, excluding the cost of the silencer.

Top Tips For Tuning:

- When you adjust your bike's suspension, do it in logical steps and keep a note of what you've done.
- If you adjust your bike's suspension and it makes no difference to the handling, it probably needs uprating by an expert.
- Virtually any machine can be made to handle well by an expert.
- Most sports bikes are plenty powerful enough for the road. You're better-off spending your money on uprating the suspension than on tuning the engine. The difference in cost between the two will buy you an aftermarket silencer as well.
- If you decide to have an engine tune, a Stage One job is the most practical for the road.
- Some people spend a lot of money tuning their engines – and gain very little power. Check with the tuner what gains you can expect.

Which Rubber Shall I Fit?

Different types and makes of tyres have a critical impact on your bike's performance. Some profiles of front tyres will make a machine steer quicker, some tyres are built for longevity, while others are produced to give maximum grip. There are hundreds of sets to choose from. Original-equipment rubber (the tyres that are fitted to a new bike) is often developed in conjunction with the bike manufacturer, but in any case will probably be suited to the type of machine. Here's an outline of what's available:

<u>Touring-Type Tyres</u> These wear well, but do not offer great grip. If you ride sedately and rack up the miles, these will suit you.

<u>Dual-Compound Tyres</u> They are softer at the edges and harder in the middle. The theory is that they wear well over distances, while giving good cornering grip.

<u>Sports Tyres</u> Being very sticky, they don't last long. However, they provide the best grip in all weathers (except for wet-weather or slick racing

Tuning Your Bike

tyres) and are essential if you intend taking part in track days. Some sports tyres are designed almost exclusively for the track so, while they offer great grip, they can also make your machine feel very nervous.

<u>Wet-Weather Race Tyres</u> Some are homologated, which means they are road-legal, although they will not fit all makes of bikes. They're incredibly sticky both in the damp and extreme cold, allowing you to ride very fast in bad conditions. They may not wear well, but they're superb fun!

DON'T OVERTYRE THE REAR

Top Tyre Tips

- Follow the manufacturers' recommendations for tyre pressures.
- Don't over-tyre the rear wheel – in other words don't fit a great, big, fat tyre that shouldn't be there. Fat rear tyres may provide a larger area for grip (which you won't need unless you're competing in World Superbikes), but they also slow down steering.
- If you repair a tubeless tyre using a roadside kit, make sure you either replace the tyre or have it professionally repaired as soon as possible.
- Take it easy for at least 50 miles after you've had a new set of tyres fitted. New tyres have a 'waxy' coating that's slippery. You can remove the shiny surface of new tyres by rubbing them down with a cloth lightly damped in petrol.
- Contact a specialist tyre company for more information.

Chapter 14: Bits & Pieces: Accessories

14
Bits & Pieces: Accessories

"I've been thinking about doing a trip lasting a couple of days, but I don't know what sort of luggage to buy. My other problem is that my bike doesn't have a centre stand, so it's difficult to work on. And I spoke to my insurance company the other day, who asked me if I had any security for my bike – and I didn't know how to reply."
James, 43 years.

After you've bought your bike and your riding gear, you can then enter the wonderful world of accessories. There are thousands of gadgets you can spend your money on, some useless, others essential. There's well-made stuff on the market, and rubbish too. So how do you know what's quality and what's not? If you're about to step into the aftermarket minefield, it's best to clue up by keeping an eye on the product tests in the bike mags (chiefly RiDE and Motor Cycle News) before you buy. This chapter covers the more sought-after, useful goodies, but it's only an introduction.

Security Devices

Thieves are a big problem. Norwich Union says that a third of all claims are for bike theft. Unfortunately motorcycles are relatively easy to nick, because a well-trained pair of hands will quickly deactivate an alarm, smash any locks and bundle your bike into the back of a van. However, that's not to say that security devices are useless. Far from it. The more deterrents you place on your bike, the less likely it is to be stolen. Here are the main devices to consider using:

<u>Disc Locks</u>: Light, portable and reasonably cheap, the disc lock is your basic anti-theft device. It's the most common form of bike security. Disc locks aren't the ultimate deterrent, but they are useful when touring or if you pop down to the shops. Unfortunately a disc lock will not stop a determined thief. The lock is secured to a brake disc and, while some makes can be smashed with a steel chisel, others have keyways that can be drilled out. The top manufacturers to look for are Abus, Kryptonite and Squire.

<u>U-Locks</u>: A good U-lock will stop opportunist thieves and joy-riders – and will go a long way to slowing down a determined thief. Although the U-lock provides more security than a disc lock, its bulk makes it far more difficult to carry on a bike. There may be space for it under the seat, but the chances are you'll have to fit a special carrying bracket or bungee it to the seat. The U-lock is most effective when it secures the bike to something like a railing or post. Failing that, it can also be used to lock together the front wheels of two motorcycles. If you have to park your bike on its own, slide the U-lock around the forks and through the front wheel, or around the swingarm and through the rear wheel.

<u>Chains</u>: By far the heaviest and bulkiest security device to carry, the chain can nevertheless be very effective at deterring thieves. However, a chain is useful for securing your bike once it's parked at home and is best used in conjunction with a ground anchor (see below). Most chains have a protective plastic coating. Two quality names are Abus and Squire.

Here are some tips when using a lock or chain:
- It's only too easy to ride away with your lock still attached...and you won't get far if you do! Tie a piece of string from the lock to the

throttle to remind you that your bike's secured.
- Don't carry a disc lock in your pocket or a chain around your shoulders. In the event of an accident they could cause serious injury.
- Secure disc locks to the top of the brake disc, and never let chains or U-locks lie on the ground, to prevent sledgehammer attacks.
- Keep a record of the key number.

Ground Anchors: A ground anchor is basically a steel loop that's either bolted or cemented into the ground. It's especially useful if you don't have a garage at home for your bike, as a quality product will provide you with something very secure to lock your bike to, although many people place anchors in their garages for extra security. Concrete-in anchors are generally more secure than the bolt-down type, but are more difficult to fit.

Alarms: Alarms are big business. Norwich Union even commissioned a third party, Sold Secure, to come up with a specification for alarms that, if fitted to your bike, will qualify you for an insurance discount. However, as Sold Secure based its specification on car systems, the complexity of these alarms does not always make them ideal for motorcycles. Some of the more popular makes are not Sold Secure approved.

Alarms are a drain on bike batteries, which can be a problem for sports bikes with lightweight batteries, but if you use your bike once or twice a week, you should have no trouble. Storing your bike over winter requires either disarming the alarm or using a trickle charger.

The serious thief will disarm an alarm in seconds once he's found it, so locating the system under the seat is a waste of time, as it will be easy to get at. Fitting the alarm under the fuel tank or behind the fairing makes it virtually impossible to access.

There have been tales of alarm-immobilisers being triggered while the bike was being ridden (hairy), but the main complaints seem to be random triggering of alarms, waterlogging, remote problems and current drain. However, a quality product, such as the Sola-larm, Datatool Series 2, Scorpio CYL 200 or Spyball 139, should be hassle-free.

Luggage

Deciding what luggage to buy depends on the type of bike you own and what sort of motorcycling you do. The less quantifiable factor is street cred – you'd no more fit a top box and hard panniers to a Yamaha R1, for example, than wear a technicolour rucksack while sitting astride your Harley-Davidson Fat Boy. You want luggage that suits your bike, but that's practical too. Here are some suggestions.

<u>Tank Bags</u>: These are an invaluable extension to your luggage, especially when touring. You place your map in the map pocket, keep ready cash in a spare pocket, store tickets, passports and other documents in the hood pocket and other bits you wish to easy access in the main compartment. There are two types of tank bag: magnetic and strap-down. Magnetic bags are easier to take off, although you have to be careful not to allow bits of metal (such as paperclips) to get between the magnets and your bike's paintwork. Consider these factors when buying a tank bag:

- Two-tier bags unzip for extra storage. A single-tier bag may have a storage area of eight litres, while some two-tiers hold up to 24 litres.
- Make sure the bag doesn't wobble around, especially if you're riding an unfaired machine.
- The magnetic flaps should hold the bag securely to the fuel tank and should fold back when carrying the bag. Some bags have a strap that goes around the headstock, so the bag won't be blown off at high speeds.
- A shoulder strap is very useful. Some bags have rucksack-type straps.
- The bag should have a waterproof cover.
- The map pocket should be a reasonable size.

<u>Rucksacks</u>: There's little to beat a rucksack for everyday use. It's one of the easiest ways to carry an extra bit of kit. It's worth buying a quality-made product if you use a rucksack regularly, as the shoulder straps often unstitch on cheaper bags.

There's also a question mark hanging over the safety of rucksacks: will they cause injury if you crash? No research has been carried out into this, but Catherine Brown, of the Spinal Injuries Unit at Stoke Mandeville Hospital, advises: "Use common sense when wearing a rucksack. Pack only light, soft things and pack them carefully for even weight distribution. Go for ones with a chest strap to lock the shoulder straps in place for extra stability. The rucksack should be long, straight and fit snugly on the back."

There are hundreds of rucksacks to choose from in camping or motorcycle shops. Consider these factors when buying one:
- A 25 to 40 litre rucksack is near optimum for biking use. If the bag is too big, it might push down on the back of your helmet and it will weigh a ton when fully packed.
- The shoulder and waist straps should be well-padded. There should be a chest strap to secure the shoulder straps.
- The shoulder straps should be chunky and heavily stitched. Weedy shoulder straps tend to become unstitched quickly.
- The straps should be easily adjustable.
- Side pockets are useful.
- The rucksack should be shower-proof.

Tail Packs: If you're happy wearing the same knickers for a week because you don't want to spoil your race replica's looks, then go for a tail pack. The tail pack straps onto the pillion seat, shouldn't affect your bike's handling, and is a great way of carrying luggage. Some tail packs are expandable, with up to 40 litres of storage space. Here are some tips when buying, and using, a tail pack:
- Try before you buy. Check the pack straps easily and securely to your bike.
- Make sure the pack is stable when fully packed and on the bike.
- A shoulder strap and carrying handle are useful. Some packs have rucksack straps.
- The pack should be reasonably waterproof and have a storm cover, which should fit tightly onto the pack.
- Tape over any bodywork where the bungee straps touch.

Throw-Over Panniers: You're off touring, have a bundle of clothes to carry, but don't want to lose too much street cred by using hard luggage – then you need throw-over panniers. Throw-overs are useful too because they can be flattened and stored neatly away when not being used. They're accessible, waterproof and comfortable for pillions. They can also be used on different makes of machines and shouldn't overly affect the bike's stability. Here's what to look for:
- The bungee straps should fit your bike. Take your bike to the shop and try fitting the panniers.

- Once fitted, the panniers should not slip sideways.
- You should be able to detach the panniers quickly.
- Make sure the panniers do not hang too close to the exhaust pipe.
- Panniers with soft material backing (such as rubber) will stop chafed bodywork. In any case, stick tape over the body work to stop chafing from the bungee straps and panniers.
- Some panniers have internal waterproof bags, while others use storm hoods. Use bin liners to guarantee your clothes remain dry.

Hard Luggage: Touring aficionados swear by hard luggage – it really is the ultimate way to carry everything you need – while top boxes are extremely useful for commuting. Many people are put off by its fuddy-duddy image but, once you've fitted the stuff, you'll wonder how you ever managed without it.

And unlike throw-overs and tail packs, hard luggage will not fall off while riding and can be locked securely to the bike. Hard luggage systems are also individually tailored to the different makes of motorcycle, so there's no chance of scuffed bodywork.

Hard luggage is made of moulded plastic that clips to frame rails or brackets attached to the bike. The securing clips are lockable, and the top box and panniers themselves are lockable. Some makes combine to give up to 130 litres of storage space, while others have waterproof inner bags so the panniers do not need to be taken off the bike when you park up overnight. The top box can make a useful pillion back rest, while the panniers may get in the way of the pillion. Find out which system is best to put on and take off your bike.

Here are some useful pointers when choosing hard luggage for your machine:
- The fitting instructions for the rails and brackets should be easy to understand, although some head scratching may be needed before carrying out the work. Your dealer can always do the job.
- Make sure the panniers and top box are easily detachable and that the locking mechanism isn't too fiddly.
- The luggage should fit securely.
- Inner waterproof bags are useful (although most hard luggage is waterproof).
- Scorch-resistant panels around the exhaust area are useful.

- The fewer seams the waterproofing material has, the more rain-resistant it will be.
- There should be reinforced eyelets for bungee straps, or Velcro straps, to secure the cover.
- If you have a luggage rack on your bike, check the cover fits over it.

Tyre Pressure Gauges

The wrong tyre pressure can seriously affect your bike's handling – and you can't rely on garage air pumps to be accurate. If the pressure in your tyres is too high, the rubber will not warm up sufficiently for it to work properly, the bike's suspension will have to work harder and the contact patch between the tyres and the road will be too small. Conversely, excessively low tyre pressure means that the tyres won't have the rigidity to keep the bike stable, the tyres may overheat and lose grip, and tyre wear will increase. Tyre pressures should be checked at least once a week.

There's a wide variety of gauges. Pencil gauges are very cheap, are easy to use and are pretty accurate, dial gauges with flexible extensions are extremely handy (some have a bleed valve so the tyre can be deflated with the gauge in place), and digital gauges are often extremely accurate. When you buy a gauge, check that you can reach the front tyre valve (brake discs make some hard to get at), that the gauge seals onto the valves with ease and that the build quality is good.

Tyre Repair Kits

You're miles from home on a cold, wet, weekend night – and you have a puncture. Basically, you're stuffed. Tubeless tyre repair kits are the means of getting home, but which should you buy?

Plug-And-Inflate: A rubber bung is glued into the hole and compressed gas cartridges inflate the tyre to around seven to 15psi. Manufacturers normally recommend riding at no more than 40mph after a repair and that a new tyre should be fitted as soon as possible. This is the most popular type of repair kit.

Foam Sealant: A canister of gas-compressed foam sealant is attached to the tyre valve by the canister hose, which screws onto the valve. Squirting the contents into the tyre seals the leak and partially inflates the tyre to around 20psi. Your recommended speed limit after the repair may be as low as 30mph. Foams sometimes allow the tyre to deflate, while sealants leave loads of gunge for the tyre fitter to clean up afterwards.

Preventative Goo: You squirt this stuff in before you even have a puncture, and it's supposed to seal punctures as they happen (so you might never even know you've had a puncture, which can be a problem). There are doubts about the safety of this system for high-speed road bikes and, like foams, it leaves a lot of mess to clear up when the tyre is changed.

Paddock Stands

Ever since the bike manufacturers decided that centre stands were unnecessary, paddock stand manufacturers have had a field day. If your bike doesn't have a centre stand, you can't lube the chain easily, check the oil level properly, clean or remove the rear wheel, or drain the engine oil. Even cleaning your bike has been made more difficult. Here are some tips when choosing a paddock stand:

- Fold-away stands can be stored neatly, but check that the stand is rigid when supporting your bike.
- The chances are you'll have to put the bike on the stand yourself, so leverage is important. The longer the supporting handle, the easier it will be to lift the bike.
- Wheels on the stand mean you can move the bike around while it's supported.
- The stand's cups, which support the bike's swingarm, should be lined with rubber to prevent damage.
- Some rear paddock stands have an adaptor to lift the front of the machine.

Intercoms

Fed up with your pillion punching you in the back, or your mates waving unintelligible sign language at you? Then it's time to buy an intercom. There are two types: the rider-to-pillion intercom and the bike-to-bike radio.

Rider-To-Pillion Systems: These are generally electronic and allow you to speak to each other at speeds of up to 80mph. However, some of the best systems are simply made of a hose that channels speech vibration straight to the other person, which can be heard at up to 100mph. Prices range from around £50 to over £250, but unfortunately do not reflect effectiveness or comfort.

Bike-To-Bike Systems: These radio intercoms are great, but useless unless your mates own the same system. Good bike-to-bike systems will work at up to 100mph and will have a useful range.

Whatever type of system you choose, remember that a comfortably-fitted headset is a must. If your helmet allows, the speakers can be placed between the helmet lining and the cheek padding. Alternatively, the speakers can be slipped between your helmet and ear after you put your helmet on. The microphone should be just touching your lips and any wires should be tucked away behind the helmet padding. Don't cut or remove any of the helmet's polystyrene lining as this will invalidate its BSI mark and it could be dangerous in a crash.

Glossary

You'll hear and read lots of words in connection with biking, and you won't have a clue what some of them mean. And that can make you feel like a right twerp. Our glossary below explains all the key biking words that you'll ever want to know.

Bearings Without bearings, your engine would quickly become scrap, as the bits of metal that move against each other would generate huge amounts of friction, then overheat and finally would partially melt and seize. Bearings prevent friction by stopping rotating pieces of metal grinding against each other. The main basic types are:
- The plain shell bearing is made of a tough alloy that can cope with huge loads and is generally found between the crankshaft and conrod big ends, and as support for the crankshaft itself.
- Ball, needle roller and taper roller bearings are made of steel balls or rollers, sandwiched between an inner and outer circle, or race. They are good at dealing with axial loads, where the load pushes at 90 degrees to the shaft. Needle rollers lie parallel to each other, while taper rollers are tapered.

Belts Harley-Davidson uses them to drive the rear wheel of their bikes, Ducati uses them to drive the valve gear of their engines. Belts are found between the crankshaft and gearbox (primary drive), gearbox and rear wheel (final drive) and crankshaft and camshaft (cam drive). Most belts are now made of ultra-tough Kevlar and have an advantage over chains in that they don't need adjusting or lubricating.

BHP "Mine puts out 140. What's yours, mate?" Brake horse power is the most talked-about aspect of any Japanese sports bike. BHP is an imperial measure of an engine's power. One horsepower is equivalent to 550 foot-pounds per second; a foot-pound is the amount of energy needed to lift one pound in weight one foot; BHP is the amount of energy needed to halt a spinning engine. If an engine is tuned for greater horsepower, it often means sacrificing mid-range power for greater top-end power.

Bottoming Out This happens when the suspension unit runs out of travel in the compression stroke. Without suspension travel the entire bike becomes rigid, which places strain on the tyres and chassis, and can lead to handling problems. Good-quality, well set up suspension does not bottom out.

Caliper The brake caliper is the component, combined with the brake disc, that stops the wheel turning. Front brake calipers are usually bolted to the forks and consist of one or more hydraulically-operated pistons inside a cast or machined metal body. When the brake lever is pulled, the pistons push toward the disc, trapping the brake pads between the pistons and disc. Most rear calipers are single-piston, while front brake calipers usually range from two to six pistons, depending on the type of bike. Generally speaking, the more brake pad area you have (six-piston calipers offer the most) the greater the stopping power and sensitivity at the brake lever.

Camshaft This is a metal shaft with lobes situated along its length. As the camshaft spins, the exhaust and inlet valves are forced open in turn by the egg-shaped lobes to allow spent gasses to escape the combustion chamber and a fresh air-fuel mix to enter. The cam lobes either bear directly onto the valves, or actuate the valves indirectly with rocker arms. The way the camshaft lobes are shaped determines when and by how much the valves open, which has a significant effect on the engine's performance.

Can You don't fit a cool-looking aftermarket silencer to your bike, you fit an end can. The can, or end can, is bikespeak.

Carbon Fibre Used in racing for its strength and light weight, and on the street for its pose value, carbon fibre products are filaments of carbon that are woven together and soaked in resin, then moulded and baked. Carbon fibre is used to make wheels, the chassis on some race bikes and fairings, but it's also used as a fashion accessory for rear huggers (mudguards), tax disc holders and frame protectors.

Carburettor Carbs blend an explosive cocktail of fuel and air, and control the amount of mix entering the cylinders by your use of the throttle. All carbs work on a venturi effect. The venturi is the narrow part of the carb, around the slide and needle, that forces air sucked into the bore to speed up. This creates a low pressure area that sucks in fuel from the float bowl. The air and fuel should then be sprayed into the engine at the optimum ratio of 14 parts of air to one part of fuel. There are two types of carburettor: constant velocity and slide. A slide carb is controlled directly by the cables attached to the throttle and gives a very direct throttle response. The CV carb uses a butterfly valve situated downstream of the slide (the valve rotates to allow more or less mixture into the engine). When the valve is opened, air pressure increases under a diaphragm and the slide is lifted.

Centre Of Gravity This is the point at which the mass of a body (for example rider and bike, or just bike) can be concentrated without altering the balance of the body. Forces such as weight and inertia are deemed to work through this point. The centre of gravity of a bike is one important factor that determines how well a bike will handle. The centre of gravity on many road bikes is often too high (which makes the bike feel top-heavy), or too far back (which makes the front wheel too light). The bike's centre of gravity changes with the addition of the rider.

Chassis The bike's skeleton, to which all the muscle and flesh are bolted. The chassis needs to be stiff to avoid flex, so most are now triangulated in structure. Sporty Japanese bikes in the 70s had a lethal combination of powerful engines and weak steel chassis that made them virtually unrideable at high speed. Then in 1987 Yamaha blew away the opposition with its revolutionary Deltabox frame, first seen in Britain in the FZR1000 Genesis. This was aluminium twin-beam and very strong, and now most Japanese sports bikes use this type. Other common chassis types are:
- Trellis, as used by Ducati, with steel tubing welded into a latticework.
- Steel double cradle, where the engine sits in a 'cradle' of two tubes.
- Single spine, where the engine hangs from a steel 'spine' that is welded to the headstock.
- No frame at all, as used by BMW. Here the engine acts as the frame.

These days the engine is often designed as an integral part of the chassis for greater strength and is then known as a 'stressed member'.

Clutch The bit between the engine and gearbox that allows you to transmit power from the engine to the drive sprocket, via the gearbox. Multiplate wet clutches consist of two drums and a series of plates that run in a bath of oil. When the clutch is engaged, the plates are clamped together so the crankshaft can rotate the gears in the gearbox. When you pull in the clutch lever, the plates are forced apart and the engine is isolated from the gearbox. Dry clutches are found on pure race bikes and a few road bikes (such as Ducatis). They are more efficient at transferring power, but are more fragile than wet clutches.

Coefficient Of Drag Used to compare the slipperiness of different machines, it's the number given for a body shape which relates its drag force to its area, air speed and air density.

Cooling By keeping an engine at a constant temperature it will run at peak efficiency. Air-cooled engines can overheat in hot weather and run too cool in the cold, as the excess heat is simply removed by metal fins around the cylinder. Suzuki's GSX-Rs of the 80s were oil-cooled, where circulating oil was cooled by a radiator. Most engines are now liquid-cooled. Here water flows around the cylinder and through the radiator, where it's cooled down, before returning to the cylinder. Liquid-cooled engines also dampen down engine noise, making is easier for manufacturers to meet strict noise emission standards.

Damping The system used in suspension to dissipate the energy of a moving part. When a suspension unit (such as a fork) compresses, the energy is stored in the spring, which would then oscillate long after it had been deflected by the road and would transmit the energy to the rest of the bike. The damping mechanism absorbs some of this energy (usually by forcing oil through small holes or past a stack of shims) to control the spring's flex. Compression damping works with the spring as it compresses, while rebound damping (the more important of the two) slows the spring's reaction. Many sports bikes have adjustable damping, but very often the range of damping that can be controlled is very limited and adjustments have little effect.

Dive When you brake hard, the front suspension compresses and the bike 'dives'. This is the result of weight transfer from the rear to the front of the machine. The degree of dive is controlled by the suspension.

Decibel (dB) This is a measure of sound volume and particularly pertinent to bikers. First, road bikes are legally silenced to produce 82dB, but many riders fit race silencers to their bikes that produce 105dB and sound great, look dead cool, but are illegal. The system is measured logarithmically, so that a 3dB increase represents a doubling in sound level. Bikers who ride a lot can suffer from hearing loss, because their ears are frequently exposed to 90dB through wind noise, which causes permanent damage to the ear drums. 120dB is the pain threshold, and fast riding often takes you into this territory. You should always wear ear plugs if you ride fast or cover long distances.

Desmodronic Valves are normally closed by a spring and valve bounce can occur at high engine speeds. Desmodronically-operated valves are opened and closed positively by camshaft lobes, which prevent bounce, especially with heavier valves. However, lighter valve steels and rev limiters have made the desmo system outdated.

Expansion Chamber The high complex, fat bit of a two-stroke's exhaust system. The shape harnesses exhaust waves to improve the flow of exhaust gasses from the cylinder and the suction of fresh gasses into the cylinder. The shape of the expansion chamber affects the engine's performance and much of the art of tuning two-strokes is knowing how best to build an expansion chamber.

Extension The travel of the suspension when it is unloaded, which may well happen when you fly over a humpback bridge.

EXUP Four-stroke engines are less reliant on exhaust pressures than two-strokes to run efficiently. However, Yamaha devised the EXUP to create the optimum pressure in the exhaust pipes at all engine speeds. The EXUP is a rotating valve, controlled by engine speed sensors and a servo motor, that alters the internal dimension of the exhaust pipe.

Fairing The moulded plastic, fibreglass or even carbon fibre material wrapped around the front of the bike that protects the rider from the elements and which makes the machine more aerodynamic (if well-designed).

Flywheel A flywheel is a rotating lump of metal, hitched to the crankshaft, that stores momentum. Single-cylinder bikes have large flywheels, as they have a long wait between power strokes, four-cylinder bikes have relatively small flywheels and two-strokes have very small ones. Large flywheels help with low-speed engine running, but prevent rapid acceleration and deceleration. A large flywheel makes an engine feel as if it has a lot of torque, which may not be the case. Old British singles feel torquey; they're not, they just have large flywheels.

Frame See **Chassis**

Fuel Injection This is a means of squirting the air-fuel mix into the engine, rather than sucking it out of a carburettor. Fuel injection can be highly efficient. Computer mapping can take into account engine speed, camshaft and piston position, manifold pressure, coolant and air intake pressures, throttle position and the rate of changed throttle position to inject the exact amount of fuel needed at any time to power the engine. Motorcycles use indirect injection, where the fuel is squirted into an inlet tract and which then travels to the combustion chamber.

G-Force The measure of acceleration and deceleration. Often used in car racing speak and less pertinent to bikers. 0 to 60mph in 2.75 seconds is equivalent to 1g. Race bikes can create 1.5g under braking, while drag bikes can pull over 2g in acceleration.

Gasket A sheet of material that seals the join between two surfaces. A gasket can be made of paper, aluminium and copper, or a composite of different materials. Gaskets should always be replaced once the seal has been broken.

Gearing This is the ratio between the engine revolution and the distance travelled by a machine in any particular gear. Gearbox ratios are fixed, but you can easily alter the overall gearing of a chain-drive bike by changing the drive (front) and wheel (rear) sprockets. Tall gearing (smaller wheel sprocket/ larger drive sprocket) will give a greater top speed if the engine is powerful enough, but it adversely affects acceleration. Short gearing (larger wheel sprocket/smaller drive sprocket) improves acceleration, but limits top speed.

Gears Bits of metal with teeth around the perimeter. The teeth of the gears mesh with one another so that one gear will turn the other and drive a shaft. Straight-cut gears are usually used in gearboxes, although helical (curved) gears are quieter-running. Paired bevel gears transmit movement through 90 degrees and are used in shaft-drive and some cam-drive mechanisms.

Head Angle See **Rake**

Headstock The front, generally very bulky part of the frame that holds the steering stem and through which huge loads are transmitted. The forks are connected to the steering stem by the yokes. The headstock of an aluminium-framed bike is cast and welded to the frame's tubes.

Hero Blobs The dangly bits of metal under the rider's footpegs that are designed to touch the Tarmac before other bits of the bike start scraping the ground with hard cornering. As footpegs are hinged, a scraped hero blob shouldn't affect the bike's stability, but if a fixed part of the machine (like the silencer) scrapes the ground a tyre could easily lose contact with the road. Scraped hero blobs are an essential part of street cred.

Horizontally-Opposed Used to describe an engine with cylinders that are opposite each other, with the crankshaft in between. BMW is famous for its 'boxer' engines. Horizontally-opposed engines are smooth because the opposing movement of the pistons balance each other out.

Hugger The rear mudguard, and a common aftermarket accessory.

Hydraulic A hydraulic system is one that uses fluid to transmit pressure. In the good old days you wondered when that frayed front brake cable would snap; these days bikes have hydraulic front brakes.

Induction That wonderful rasping roar some bikes make when you open the throttle, as air is forced into the carbs. It's also the term used to describe the air-fuel mixture being sucked into the cylinder, and many sports bikes now use forced air pressure (ram air) and tuned air boxes to enhance induction. The inlet tract is made up of the carburettor, manifold and the inlet port. The length of the inlet tract is crucial to an engine's performance; slow-revving bikes like long inlet tracts, high-revving bikes short ones.

Injector A pressurised nozzle, most commonly used in fuel injectors to squirt fuel into the cylinders.

Internal Combustion Engine An engine in which heat is developed in the cylinder rather than outside (a steam engine is an external combustion engine). In 1885 Gottlieb Daimler built an internal combustion engine that was to power the first motorcycle up to 7.5mph.

Jet A small hole through which fuel or oil passes. Jetting up carbs means fitting jets with larger holes to allow more fuel to pass through.

Kevlar A petroleum-based synthetic fibre made by Du Pont that is massively strong. It's used in bullet-proof jackets, belts as in motorcycle belt drives, as an anti-abrasion protective skin in bike clothing and as a strengthener in helmets. Often so little is used in protective bike clothing that it's worthless, but the name sells products.

Layshaft The shaft in the gearbox that lies parallel to the main shaft, and on which the clutch is located.

Lean This is when the air-fuel mixture passing into the engine rises beyond the ideal 14:1 ratio. Excessive air weakens the mixture and can lead to detonation in four-strokes and seizure in two-strokes.

Liner Commonly a steel cylinder that slots into the alloy barrel of an engine and forms the cylinder bore. A wet liner is one which is in contact with the engine's coolant and allows the cylinders to be placed close together.

Master Cylinder Hydraulic brakes and clutches have master cylinders, operated by the brake and clutch levers, and rear brake pedal. The master cylinder is basically a syringe that increases the pressure of the hydraulic fluid, which, in the case of the brakes, forces the brake caliper pistons towards the disc. Rubber brake hoses become elastic with time, giving a spongy feel to the brakes, which is why many people fit steel braided hoses. Rubber brake hoses also tend to expand slightly when placed under pressure, while steel braided hoses do not. Brake fluid tends to absorb water and, as water boils under pressure, water-contaminated brake fluid leads to fading brakes.

Mixture The air-fuel mix that goes into the engine from the carburettors. The mixture needs to be around 14 parts air to one part fuel, while the fuel burns most efficiently when it's evenly distributed as very fine droplets (atomised) in the air.

Monoshock The single shock absorber that controls the swingarm in an attempt to keep one tyre in contact with the ground for as long as possible. Most modern bikes have rear monoshocks (some have twin shocks), although BMW notably uses a monoshock up front. Rear monoshocks are usually attached to the frame at one end and either directly to the swingarm, a linkage system, or cantelever at the other. The linkage system improves the ride and control of the rear wheel, while a monoshock allows more wheel travel than a twin-shock system.

Multigrade Oil Multigrades are designed to maintain their viscosity over a wide range of temperatures (so they can be used year-round) while monogrades need to be changed depending on the seasons.

Needle The needle in a carburettor is a thin, tapered rod that alters the aperture of the needle jet as it rises and falls. The taper ensures that the amount of fuel passed into the engine increases correctly as the throttle is opened. Below ¼ throttle, the pilot jet and slide cutaway do most of the work; between ¼ and ¾ the needle jet is the main influence; and above ¾ the main jet takes over.

Nikasil This is a very thin plating of nickel and silicon carbide applied to alloy cylinder bores that makes for a highly durable surface. The electrochemical process is used mainly on two-stroke engines but, because it is much lighter than conventional cylinder liners, it's becoming increasingly used in four-strokes.

Nitro Nitromethane is a highly flammable fuel that liberates huge amounts of oxygen and increases power by as much as 70 per cent. It's beloved by drag racers.

Nitrous Nitrous oxide is a gas that does much the same job as nitro, although it's also used as an anaesthetic. It's stored in a bottle, so is not convenient to carry around.

Nyloc A nut with a nylon insert that stops loosening due to vibration.

Octane Rating This is the measure of resistance a fuel has to detonation and pinking. High octane fuels do not offer more performance than lower octane fuels, and running a high octane fuel in a low-compression engine is a complete waste of money. This is because the octane-enhancing additives inhibit combustion, so some of the fuel will not burn.

Oil A wonderful liquid that forms a film between the metal bits, which stops them destroying each other. Its properties break down with age and use, so the oil should be changed as recommended.

Overhead Camshaft The OHC is the most common method of controlling the opening and closing of the cylinder valves. The OHC is situated directly above the valves and the lobes, which are in almost direct contact with the valve stems, open and close the valve very accurately. In the old days the cam lobes were often situated just above the crankshaft and operated the valves via pushrods.

Power This is the rate at which work is carried out in the engine, while torque is the force developed. Power equals torque x rpm. If torque is the strength of each combustion, power is the cumulative effect of these bangs.

Power Band This is the range of engine speed that delivers useful power. The rule of thumb states that your engine can have a wide spread of power, or a lot of power bunched up in one area, but not both. That's the reason why, when your engine is tuned, you gain power in one area and lose it in another. Power is sapped by the engine's internals (reciprocating mass), the gearbox, the chain or shaft drive, and the wheels. Thus power measured at the engine is always greater than power measured at the rear wheel.

Preload Usually referred to as the compression on the springs in your bike's shock and forks. The spring preload is the load that must be exceeded before the spring begins to compress. There is a common misconception that increasing the preload stiffens the spring; it does not, it simply increases the loading required to compress the spring. Ideally, for the suspension damping to work most effectively, you want your preload set as soft as possible.

Radial Tyres Most bike tyres are now radial. This means that the plies (the material sections that lie under the rubber) are at right angles to the bead, allowing for greater grip, longer wear and lower sidewalls than cross-ply tyres.

Rake Nothing to do with the garden and everything to do with your bike's stability and steering. The rake is normally measured as the angle between the steering head and the vertical. On road bikes it's generally 24° to 27°, although some sports bikes go down to 23° and some customs may go up to 30°. A shallow rake generally offers greater stability and a better self-centering effect of the front wheel, while a radical angle (say 23°) will make the bike lively and steer quickly. However, rake in itself does not determine stability; trail does this, although the two are in effect linked.

Rebound Damping Rebound damping controls the rate at which the suspension unit returns to its normal position. See Damping.

Rev Limiter Used to stop mechanical vandals totally destroying their engines by over-revving them. The rev limiter cuts in around 500rpm above the rev counter's red line and prevents the spark plugs doing their job.

Rotor The name given to the steel or cast iron disc of a disc brake.

SAE The SAE on a bottle of oil means it meets the standards defined by the American Society of Automotive Engineers.

Scratching What loonies do when they go out for a blast on their race replicas. It means they corner so fast that the bike's extreme lean angle causes parts (generally footpegs) to scrape along the ground.

Screen The transparent plastic incorporated into the top of the fairing that allows you to see ahead when you've got your head down on a sportster, or which you sit behind on a tourer. Badly-designed screens can cause turbulence around your helmet and are extremely noisy. Some manufacturers, like BMW, offer electrically-operated screens that can be raised or lowered at the push of a button, while some others can be adjusted by hand.

Shim A piece of metal of a certain thickness that is used to achieve a desired distance between two mechanisms. The most commonly-referred-to shims are those used to adjust the intake and exhaust valves, although engine shaft or gear trains may also be shimmed.

Shock Absorber See **Monoshock.**

Silencer The big lump at the back end of the exhaust pipe that stops you being nicked for making too much noise. Also known as an end can, it contains baffles that deaden the noise.

Spring Rate The force needed to compress the spring by one unit of length. There are different types of spring: linear, where the rate remains constant; double rate, where the rate increases once the spring reaches a certain point; and progressive, where the rate increases progressively.

Sprung Mass The part of the motorcycle which is supported by the suspension, for example the engine, frame, bodywork and rider. The unsprung mass is those parts not supported by the suspension, for example the wheels, brakes, transmission and moving parts of the suspension. To keep the wheels in contact with the ground, the unsprung mass needs to be as light as possible in relation to the sprung mass. The sprung-unsprung ratio of a bike is crucial to its handling.

Swingarm The pivoted section of frame that holds the back wheel and allows it to move up and down over the road surface. Some swingarms are braced for extra rigidity. The swingarm's movements are controlled by the shock.

Tachometer Also known as rev counter or tacho, this measures the engine revolutions. Most rev counters read up to 10 per cent optimistically.

Electronic rev counters are more accurate than cable-operated ones.

Tank Slapper A nasty, terrifying moment when the lock-to-lock movement of the handlebars is so violent that you cannot control it. Tank slappers are most common on bikes with radical steering geometry, although they can happen on any machine. Steering dampers are not a cure, but iron out the worst effects. If you suffer a tank slapper, do not throttle off and do not try to brake.

Telelever Part of BMW's system of front suspension system, the Telelever is a wishbone that's attached to the engine and forks, and supports the monoshock.

Torque This is a twisting force and the term is used to express the twisting force developed on the crank. Torque is best seen as the power of each combustion bang and is measured in pound-feet in Britain; in the Imperial system, torque and power are numerically equal at 5252rpm. So-called torquey engines (like old British singles) are generally just underpowered things with huge flywheels.

Trail The distance of the centre of pressure of the tyre's contact patch with the ground from the point where the steering axis meets the ground. Generally speaking, the steering is heavier and more stable if the trail is increased.

Valve In a four-stroke, the poppet valve (shaped a bit like a mushroom) is the means for regulating the flow of gasses into and out of the combustion chamber. The valves are opened and closed by cams, pushrods, rockers or Ducati's desmodronic arrangement.

Weave A bike weaves when it follows an S-shaped course. This is usually triggered by suspension wallow.

Further Reading

Bike (circ: 85,000, monthly) – Glossy, general-interest mag with news, road tests and features.

Biking Times (circ: 30,000, monthly) – New on the market, with news, features and road tests, and catering for bikers aged 30-plus.

Classic Bike (circ: 55,000, monthly) – Deals mainly with British and European classics, but with a smattering of early Japanese stuff.

Fast Bikes (circ: 30,000, monthly) – Crash-and-burn antics, wheelies, stoppies and the odd road test.

Motor Cycle News (circ: 140,000, weekly) – The latest news, road tests, product tests, features and some sports reporting.

Motorcycle Sport and Leisure (circ: 30,000, monthly) – Aimed at the older biker and featuring everything from scooters to hyperbikes.

Performance Bikes (circ: 80,000, monthly) – Caters for the yoof who's growing up. Slightly laddish, slightly sane.

RiDE (circ: 75,000, monthly) – Bags of useful information about everything you need to know, with excellent product tests, an accent on second-hand machines and road tests of new bikes.

Superbike (circ: 70,000, monthly) – Laddish, with centrefold topless totty draped over bike, but also contains road tests and sports reports.

Index

abrasion tests, 38

bearings, 157
belts, 157
biker haunts, 62
body armour, 34, 35, 44
boots, 37, 45
brakes
    calipers, 98, 158
    dive, 160
    horsepower, 157
    master cylinder, 164
    pads, 98
    rotor, 167
budget bikes, 16
bump-starting, 94

camshaft, 158, 166
carbon fibre, 158
carburettor, 158
centre of gravity, 159
centre stands, 92
chains, 94, 95
chassis, 159
clutch, 160
coefficient of drag, 160
cold, effects of, 41
commuter bikes, 20
Compulsory Basic Training, 7
custom bikes, 19

decibel (dB), 33, 161
desmodronic, 161
disabled bikers (NABD), 117

electrically-heated gear , 42, 43

engine tuning
    Stage One, 143
    Stage Two, 143
expansion chamber, 161
EXUP, 161

fairing, 161
ferries abroad, 74
fluids, brake and clutch, 98
flywheel, 162
fuel
    fuel-air mix, 164, 165
    injection, 161
    octane rating, 166

G-force, 162
gasket, 162
Gatso cameras, 53
gears, 162
gloves, 36, 46
grey imports, 26

headstock, 163
helmets, 32
horizontally-opposed, 163
hugger, 163
hydraulic, 163

induction, 163
injector, 164
insurance, 55, 73
intercoms, 154

jet (carburettor), 164

Kevlar, 64

layshaft, 164
leather suits, 34
licence, 8
liner, 164
luggage
    hard, 152
    rucksacks, 150
    soft, 149
    soft panniers, 151
    tail packs, 151
    tank bags, 150

maintenance tips, 101
master cylinder, 164
motorway riding, 54

needle, 165
nitro, 165
nitrous, 165
noise levels and safety, 33
nyloc, 166

official imports, 23
Oil, engine
    changing, 97
    definition, 166
    multigrade, 165
    standards, 167

paddock stands, 93, 154
parallel imports, 24
pillions, 72
police
    attitudes, 51
    bike haunts, 55
    dealing with, 52, 58
    foreign, 71, 78
    motorways, 54

power band, 166
protective clothing, 31
provisional licence, 6
pursuit test, 8

race replicas, 16
rake, 167
retros, 18
rev limiter, 167
riding tips (advanced)
    backside, 119
    body language, 120
    braking and turning, 124
    braking approach, 123
    contact points, 119
    countersteering, 125
    cutting corners, 131
    front brake use, 123
    hard braking, 124
    hidden dangers, 132
    knee down, 129, 130
    leaning the bike, 128
    machine limitations, 127
riding tips (beginners)
    common accidents, 114
    conspicuous, 116
    contact points, 106
    cornering, 112, 113, 114
    escape routes, 107
    filtering, 115
    mental approach, 103
    overtaking, 110, 111
    physical approaches, 106
    relaxing, 104
    repeat accidents, 105
    road position, 111, 114, 116
    steering, 113
    vanishing point, 113
    vision, 107, 108, 109

problem-solving, 133
throttle control, 121, 122
vision, 131
weight distribution, 128
road race meetings, 65

scooters, 20
scratching, 55, 167
screen, 167
second-hand bikes, 27
security devices, 148
shim, 168
shows, 63
silencers, 142, 158, 168
speeding, 50, 53
sports bikes, 14
sports-tourers, 17
sprung mass, 168
suspension
    bottoming out, 158
    damping, 160, 167
    extension, 161
    lean angle, 127
    monoshock, 138, 165
    preload, 166
    settings, 139
    spring rate, 168
    telescopic forks, 139
    tuning, 141
    twin shocks, 139
swingarm, 168

tachometer, 168
tank slapper, 134, 169
telelever, 169
theory test, 7
thermal clothing, 44
tinnitus, 33
torque, 169

tourers, 19, 72
touring
    accommodation, 75
    distances, 75
    France, 76
    Italy, 77
    luggage, 75
    pillions, 72
    Spain, 78
    Switzerland, 77
    travel documents, 73
track days
    circuits, 87
    common problems, 85
    machine preparation, 82
    mental preparation, 81, 83
trail, 169
trailies, 18
training
    basic, 8
    insurance and, 57
tyres
    confidence in, 127
    pressure gauges, 153
    radial, 167
    repair kits, 153
    tips, 145
    types of, 144

V-twins, 16, 17
valve, 169
VASCAR, 54
visors, 47

weave, 169
winter suits, 44

Comments

If you've got any comments, anecdotes, advice, moans and groans, or in fact anything at all you want to say about your born-again biking experiences, we'd love to hear from you. Write to us at::

>Back In The Saddle
>Caring Books
>PO Box 1565
>Glasgow G46 6SX

Or email us at: caringbooks@backinthesadlle.co.uk

Further Copies

You can buy further copies of **Back In The Saddle** by sending a cheque for £14.99 (inc p&p) to the address below. (Don't forget to include your name and address.)

>Caring Books
>PO Box 1565
>Glasgow G46 6SX

Web Site

Visit our web site: www.backinthesaddle.co.uk

Stadium
2 Loxham Road
Chingford
London E4 8SE
Tel: 0208 531 9026

Pyramid Plastics

Bespoke Accessories Since 1986

Huggers **Seat Cowls** Belly Pans **Screens**
Headlight Covers **Undertrays** Extenda Fendas
Tank Shields Handlebar Screens **Yoke Protectors**

Tel: 01427 810473

Rush me a copy of your FREE brochure and fact sheet detailing kit for my bike
- My bike..
- Year..

Name..
Address..
....
...................................Postcode................................

Send to: Pyramid Plastics Limited,
           Britannia Works, Beaumont Street,
           Gainsborough, Lincolnshire DN21 2EN

FREE ADVICE - CALL STEVE ROSS 08000 285978

INJURED?
NOT YOUR FAULT?

FREEPHONE
COLIN McKENZIE
AND
STEVE ROSS
08000 285 978
NOW!

Instant free advice so you know where you stand

- What you must do!
- How to maximise compensation!
- How to get back on the road!
- What you can claim!

GET A GRIP
DON'T DELAY
GET IT SORTED NOW
NO WIN - NO FEE

But why wait until you've had an accident?
Find out more in our free Newsletter *BikeFocus*
To get your FREE copy ring
08000 285978

GO FOR EXPERIENCE AND RESULTS

Steve says:

"After being injured in an accident, get a solicitor, preferably a motorcycling solicitor and definitely a personal injury solicitor. Ask searching questions - treat us like any other piece of kit. Make sure they can do what you need. Look for legal qualifications, proven track record and genuine experience. Choose carefully. Remember the general rule in most cases is loser pays. Go for someone who will make the guilty person pay, not someone who will take a cut out of your compensation. If anyone else wants to take some of your compensation as part of their fee, speak to us for FREE. We aim to be one of the best bits of kit that you've got."

MOTORCYCLIST INJURY UNIT
WOLFERSTANS

www.wolferstans.com ~ email: pi@wolferstans.com

FREE ADVICE - CALL COLIN McKENZIE 08000 285978